# Whispers From Within

Special thanks to Helen, Bonnie and Chrissie

for their encouragement & support.

# Whispers From Within

John Harrison

Published by Albion Press
54 Hollingdean Road, Brighton, BN2 4AA

# Cradle Me

Cradle me
In your arms
And hold me tight

Cradle me
When I'm too exposed
And I haven't got the fight

Cradle me
And *tell me*
"Everything's alright"

Cradle me
So I won't have to suffer
The night

Cradle me
And *make*
Everything alright

Cradle me
With a softness
Of delight

Cradle me...

And not just tonight

# CONTENTS

An Introduction to the Author:-

I am thirty nine years old. As a child I faced all types of child abuse. And throughout my life and up until the present day I have faced neglecting and abusing attitudes or discrimination. But worst of all for me now is it's from the very systems that should have been helping and supporting me.

I was born in Wellington Hospital on the outskirts of Devon in 1970. The youngest of four boys I was raised by both my parents. We lived in Sheldon a small village in Devon until I was eleven. Sheldon basically consisted of a row of council houses with a few farms and houses dotted about. The nearest town was about ten miles away. It is here that I would receive the main cause of my problems later in life which was caused by Child Abuse. I was abused in every way you can be Physically, Emotionally and Sexually. Although I must add I was not Sexually Abused by a member of my family. That's not to say that their treatment of me was not significantly damaging because it was.

While living in Devon the abuse I faced was from being regularly around six people, all of which hurt me. Including my Parent's, who had done things like hitting me with a stick, I'd also been hit with a knife aged three which scarred me for the rest of my life, I had my leg broke at the age of four. My brothers when they weren't hurting each other were hurting me, setting fire to my feet and other cruel games they played. I had nowhere to run, and no one too run too.

On top of this the other person (my dad's work mate) sexually abused me. One sick glimpse of him in my head is, of him holding me down as he laughed in my face, as I struggled to stop him or get away. Just before I was eleven my parents split up. My mother myself and two of my brothers moved away. We moved to Andover a small town in Hampshire. My farther, I didn't know where he was. But he did stay in the Devonshire area. Now this is the main point where my main Mental Block started. And this would remain so for the next twenty or so years.

To explain this next important part of my life is very difficult, but I will try. There was a moment after recently moving to Andover, when my Mother and One or Two of my Brothers were speaking of something that they had done,

1

setting fire to my feet, they laughed. I tried to remember this. At that time it would not have been that far back. But I couldn't remember. It felt strange I cannot describe it. Next, something was mentioned about when I was hit with a knife. I heard my brother say "Yeah but you shouldn't have hit him with a knife". What happened to that eleven year old next would shape many things to come.

I carried on like nothing had happened not even thinking it strange that I couldn't remember. And I carried on with life, on a couple of occasions when a flash back occurred relating to being sexually abused. It was like I thought. "Why am I thinking this?" "There is something wrong with me", and the person was not someone I knew now or even recognised as someone who was real. It was no longer something that did happen, but some strange things that was in my head. Strange as that may sound that's exactly how it was. And others who have been abused have had the same sort of experience too.

So all the above, it was like it all never happened. And I believed I'd had a good child hood and I was lucky unlike some. Of which people pointed out many a time. I believed that my mum and dad had split up because of my dad's infidelity. But, it all did happen, and though my mind was or seemed blank. It was all in there and worse still the affects of it do things psychologically to you. But I knew no different. Sadly at no point was I given the right help. If I had there would have been no block. And things would have been very different.

So I went on messed up deeper than you can imagine. And in which needs so much more detail and discussion that these brief pages can say. And not even knowing it I went through life believing in my peers, my Mum, brothers, my Dad and missing him terribly so. But all because of what I would say programming. I was so messed up. Sorry still am. And my so called child hood remained hidden from me until my early thirties. I said programming because what I and others have had makes brainwashing not look or sound as bad. It's so deep, so fundamental and its affects are countless and numerous.

I can do something Good, something to help others and yet I can feel guilty or selfish. And I don't usually get that nice feeling you should. Years of this type of stuff of being punished for being good, Let alone being punished for being naughty, has done great damage to me even now. If your parent goes to hit you with the stick, defending yourself is not an option. Whatever was going to happen is just about to get even worse. It's like... you dare defend yourself, like you're somebody. Like you deserve better?

The person who sexually abused me was trying to give me a cake once when I was little. I didn't want it to me (for obvious reasons) it felt dirty. I was made to feel like the most ungrateful spoilt child in the whole world, Worthless. You get that a lot. And again there is a life time especially as a child of this. So with this and more relationships would always be difficult. Long-term ones, Proper, loving caring ones. Ones I would learn to run a mile away from without realising. This I later learned was a safety mechanism within me, because inside I feared it.

Growing up, girls I loved them but my relationships with them were so badly affected, and then later on with women too. Physical for me either involved being hit as a child or being abused sexually there was little if any type of touch involved other than that. Please never under estimate that physical touch in non sexual cuddles and the good that it does. I struggled for many years with this type of touch. It was so uncomfortable for me at best. It's so painful when you begin to realize what is and has been so missing profoundly in your life. There again is so much messed up stuff I could tell you about this, but for here and now, you can imagine it was unpleasantly all disturbing and extremely damaging. Through one thing and another, neglect, abuse it all continued, though the sexual abuse did stop.

In my early twenties after starting working on building sites I eventually became a builder. I started my own business and after a few years about four I drove head long into it. Basically if truth be known my business was all I had. I was so withdrawn no matter how I came across to others, which included people thinking I was confident. I know that because year's later people told me this is how they looked on me at that time. But deep down it couldn't have been further from the truth. I had no real social life. For a few years earlier and at the time I turned thirty some Family that were around became ill. I was struggling myself as well, and pressure yes most I put on myself in the end it all caught up with me. I started not being able to work as regular which in turn gave me financial problems and yes stress. In the end I started getting severe Panic attacks. And this is where it all started to turn for the worse with myself and Doctors in general.

It was extremely embarrassing at first going to the Dr in the mess I was. And basically being a young man who could not cope, who was falling to pieces. And who was scared of what was happening to him. I started thinking and feeling some strange things. And it wasn't easy (though I did) to tell the Dr's what I was going through. The first problem I came across. My problems weren't taken seriously enough. I got told "your just stressed you should take up football or something". As if I was wasting his or their time. And it just, like my health never got better. In fact in the years that followed it got a lot worse.

At first despite what the Dr's were saying I did just what they said. I in my thirties began to be so ill I was unable to work anymore. Then when I was referred to the Mental Health Services they didn't take it or me seriously too. The Mental Health Service, I found out years later, were well aware of my child hood, even if I wasn't. But when it did start to come out in me, did they give me any help? Did they show me any compassion at least? NO. They unbelievably used it as a reason and excuse to NOT see me and NOT help me. I cannot tell you what that did and does to me even now. I was alone as I had always been. People, this alone is unacceptable.

Right back to and from 1996 things had got a lot worse while trying to get the right help. And having not got the help I needed I had to turn to private healthcare. But I couldn't afford it. I did it for as long as I could but then the Private Psychologist got me referred back to my local CMHT. They then couldn't deny me any help, or that I needed some. So they reluctantly saw me which I believe was another problem with them at the beginning. And then they just got it all wrong. Over the next few years I would be in hospital four times. I started standing up for myself from about 1996. Taking my issues with those involved straight away, and when that was no good taking it to people higher up and outside the organisation (NHS). I went through all the outside bodies and internal ones regarding making complaints for over a decade. But know one helped or listened properly.

And that's what led to me campaigning for true accountability within the system, writing to MP's, The Prime Minister even the Royal Family and Her Majesty the Queen herself. I'm still trying to be heard, which at the end of this book I will go into what I started to do to achieve this from 2008 but especially in 2009. But it also nicely brings me to this book and my writing.

I used to write when I was younger and playing the guitar, I used to write songs. Dreaming, like many, of being in my own band writing and singing. To put it simply sooner or later it had to stop. Because I'd got dermatitis from the building work and so had to stop playing the guitar. The knock on affect of this was to stop writing songs and so stop writing all together. **"Who is the Pest?"** is the only Poem from that period in here. As I discussed above there was a point I no longer could work. Going through all the things I was with no proper help I was going out of my mind. And I decided to document how I felt, asking questions of those around me, of myself and trying to find answers. So I started writing a journal.

The journal consisted of diary entries, prose, poetry, gibberish, all sorts. After I had been writing in it for a while I saw that it could be a book. But I later realized that it was too much for one book. After much pulling out of the hair I decided to take out the Poetry and most of the Prose and do this my first book. I again will go into more detail about that at the end of the book. Especially as its importance became more obvious to me in 2009, where some very significant things happened and indeed still are.

This introduction is to just give you a glimpse of the kind of issues that I faced and still do. To make sense of that what led me to write, and led me to what I write about. The layout of this book is as follows. I put several Poems and Prose in a section and then end that section by doing a description of some of the previous items, picking out some of particular interest and significance to me. I have done this to let you read them first before I have my say or take on them. There is an exception just because I did the right up and it complements the Poem and won't get in your way as you read it, **"Questionable Anger"** being the one.

The books intentions like my own, is to show creativity and to take positivity from and through all of this, Airing The Silence, all the types of Silence and yes promoting me, us and the cause through Poetry & Prose and in doing so.

*Raise Awareness of Child Abuse and its Consequences in Later Life.*

5

Lost in the mind
Only in the mind
Can you find, the way
A Journey like no other
But remember
You have to be ready
For this Journey
To have a chance
Of the destination
You really want
Yourself


Good Luck

# Who is the Pest?

Men say "this animal is a pest"
Some say insects are a pest
There is really only the one
Mankind himself he is the one

We destroy everything in a stride
Animals and insects have to hide
Here comes man and his vision
Making earth the ultimate prison

If you want to clean up the place
Meet with each other face to face
Stop destroying and face the fact
The pest is man and his acts

If anything stands in mans way
We wipe them out and they pay
When you walk amongst his kind
Gotta look over your shoulder, all the time

*This is one of my very early Poem's*

# Emotions

It comes in waves
Emotions of slaughter
The pain sinks like a stone
Anger rises like the sun
Love comes and goes
Like passing winds
Jealousy builds up like a storm
And explodes like thunder
Misery is prolonged
Like the inevitable
The heart is a precious place
Emotions fight for a space
Happiness you cannot reach
Like the stars up above
Tears well up and flow
Like a river
But only on the inside
Sadness is a bottomless pit
And desire is like a fire
Emotions of how you feel
Are what they become

# Outside and Inside

The world outside seems busier and busier
As I stand and look out my window
As I stand and watch it all go by
Sometimes a tear wells up in my eye
As I feel I can't join in
And there's so much I'm missing
I try, oh how I try to get rid of this feeling
It seems to follow me even when I am sleeping
To some I might seem quite alright
They don't realize how I have to fight
The battle feels never ending
I just hope that one day I will win
But from where I stand in the here and now
I don't think I've got to grips with it right now
Sometimes I feel I've had enough
All this battling is too tough
Some days it's too tough for me to bear
And I feel a deep feeling of despair

# Time

Time stands still for no one
You've just got to do and get on
Sometimes it seems faster and faster
The pace just seems to blast ya
It makes you think you're not immortal
And we are, so mortal
What is gone is gone for good
Don't let that be misunderstood
You must make the most of now
Before you take your final bow

## What is Love?

Mathematics cannot calculate it
Nor can it accumulate it
Is it an emotion or a force?
Is it chemical or mystical?
What is it? Is it a sickness?
Is it real? So many think they feel
So is it a feeling? is it a real thing?
Can you touch love as it touches you?
Is there an answer to the question?
Or could we not understand?
Is it imagination? or a vain thing?
How do you know when it's there?
How can you be aware?
Does it consume you and then leave you?
Or is that love not true

Love just is, that's all you can know

## Why?

Why when I speak, you do not hear me?
Why can you not see what's so plain to see?
Sometimes I feel invisible
I don't know is it possible?
How can I make you understand?
So we can start to make a plan
To get me back into this world

The very first Poem **"Who is the Pest?"** is the only Poem from when I used to play the guitar and write songs, written when I was around twenty.

The other five Poems were done just before I started the Journal I talked of earlier. These were written at the time I tried to get help through the Mental Health Services. And I think through what I wrote you can see glimpses of how I felt and was feeling. These things need to come out. And after being suppressed by myself and others it seeped out in many ways but most obviously as you can see through Poetry. Which of all the ways it came out, was the safest and most productive, maybe not so much at the time but afterwards, looking back. The short Poem **"Why?"** is particularly important as it shows how I felt even when I spoke I still was not heard or listened too. Sadly this would not change indeed this would only get worse **"Outside and Inside"** is very sad especially since its true. I began to feel very low and this you can also see in the Poem **"Time"** even the desperation I felt because at times (then just turned thirty) I felt like life was already over, there was no point and what was worse is... I hadn't even started... to live.

I have tried to keep what is in this book in the general order it came out wherever possible but I have had to move things around a bit to fit them in these pages better. But the general layout is reasonably in sequence. What you will now see has been taken out of The Journal of which I spoke about in the introduction which I began to write. It started on an A5 notepad and the first lines were...


POSITIVE IS THE CREATION OF LIFE ITSELF
NEGATIVE IS THE DESTRUCTION OF ONES SELF AND OTHERS


*And so, on we go*


11

## There is no Fight

Evil and Negativity is like a Fire
It is ignited, it burns and it Rages
And in it you can see Beauty
But when the Fuel has gone
It is extinguished
As with Evil and Negativity
It needs fuel to Rage
Deny it that Fuel
And it can no longer be
So you don't need to fight it
It itself is on self destruct

## Door to Life

I had shut the door to life
To defend myself
Life came through the door
And I could not cope, or handle it
Because I did not accept things
Therefore they overwhelmed me
And my heart and mind shut down
And I felt lost
And now I have to start again
It is frightening
I have no reference in real life
Everything is new and confusing

# The Pond of Life

I used to go to the lakes to watch or feed the ducks. And this day I did not realize that the swans had three signets. They were around the corner. There was one goose in the lake and it was miles away from the swans but this swan turned and started heading towards this goose. In its expression as in its body motion through the water and its wing's and neck. You could see the swan's intentions towards this goose. And even the way it was thrusting through the water. And it chased the goose out of the water. I then realized and saw the signets I knew why and what it was doing. You see when you look at other animals and you see their actions sometimes it may not seem nice but there is good reason for their preservation that this is the way of things. Unlike mankind who is so called advanced, far too much for his own good. It is not enough that one would kill his brother for food. It is that he would kill for his possessions too. WHY? There is a word WANT. That he has you want is enough.

While watching the swans chasing the geese, of which I did feel sorry for the geese, something funny happened. The swans were together and this little female duck went straight through the middle of the swans. And the swans didn't react. Yes obviously the swans don't see them as a fret to themselves or their young. And I thought that in this hierarchy there a duck might seem lowly. But it was better to be a duck than to be a goose. It was funny watching this little duck moving without a care in the world doing something that a goose at least twice its size could not. And for a while a goose would try and get in the water each time again the swans would chase them out, while the ducks do as they have always done.

I suppose the moral of this story for me is in life it is better to be a duck in the pond of life. As beautiful, majestic and powerful as a swan is the constant showing of you being on top of this hierarchy and expelling this energy, or the geese and this confrontation, and finally the duck. Doing what you do to fulfil what you are with less confrontation with others. That is the way to be. So if you see them, spare a thought they are not lowly. They are not simple ducks they understand what life really is without education as we would know. And are they not better off for it? IN THE POND OF LIFE.

# Yourself

It's like a Jigsaw it doesn't fit together yet
And you don't recognize the picture
You think that there are pieces missing
And that maybe some pieces are not the right ones
You can't move on until it fits together
And that maybe if you are able to put it together
You still wouldn't recognize the picture
YOURSELF

# Onwards and Upwards

You realize that the staircase to recovery has countless steps that seem to go on forever. And slipping back means sliding down a slide that gets faster and faster. If you don't get back on track soon you can so often end up back where you started. So no matter how far you have come. You know it's a short trip back. And it's a fact that's hard to handle, and it can be demoralizing and soul destroying. So you can't dwell on it. But this fact is not easy to cope with. It makes you feel, will I ever see the top? You know it is there as it is for everyone. I can't tell you how I would feel or how much it means to me. Just to stand at the top and truly escape from this ball and chain that I am dragging around with me.

# Mankind's True Legacy (part one)

Starving your Brother so that you may have more than you're ever need. Taking advantage of someone in the name of Love. Misrepresenting people so that you can suppress or destroy them. Deny the truth so that you can tell you're lie and make others believe it is the truth. Dropping bombs and killing them with your peace. Giving Justice, but only if they can afford it. Denying people their way of life because only yours is right. Tell us black is white, Day is night, so much so that in the end we believe the unbelievable. If you are different you are weird. Believe in something else then you are mad. And countless other things, that's not good reading. I write this it sounds like I am a Psychotic Depressive doesn't it? I'M NOT. It in some cases where each is used is a reality we cannot escape from. That we try is why it still happens to us or from us. To deny a problem is to never solve it. That is the truth. There are many beautiful things in you me all of us. I would like to write it. Call it Mankind and his True Legacy part two the Final chapter. Can I? Can you? I will end on a command from Picard in Star Trek after he gives his order. It is to you me all of us. MAKE IT SO. Mankind and his true Legacy, may it override part one and be the fulfilment of part two. Write it, teach it, be it. And it will be… our Legacy.

# YOU ARE ME

I WILL ALWAYS LOVE YOU
I WILL ALWAYS WANT YOU
I WILL ALWAYS NEED YOU
I WILL ALWAYS BE WITH YOU
BECAUSE YOU ARE ME
AND THAT'S WHAT YOU MEAN TO ME

# Past, Present and Future

Sorry is a nice word but it does not undo. Forgiveness does not put it right. As good as they are and can feel to you. You see if you have problems or bad times. You must realize it doesn't help you or anyone if you live in the past. You cannot truly live there for it does not exist, does it? Remnants of it in you yes, but it is the past that has gone. You cannot change the past. No matter what you think and feel about it. No matter how much you want or would like to anytime afterwards. You in wanting to or trying to, will only do more damage to yourself or others around you. In the end you need to accept and realize this to be able to move on. And you do need to. It is exactly what it says THE PAST. It does not have to be the present and the future. If you realize this you can make a change and say to yourself. The past I cannot change, the present I can do something about and if you do that you will help your future.

As for the future you cannot exist there neither because it does not exist yet, does it? Again no matter how much you'd like it too or want it, it isn't here yet. And if you realize that in life the possibilities of what will, might or does happen are infinite truly so. And not in a negative way but no matter what you plan for the future as best you're plans are a lot can happen to change you and your situation, by the time you get to the future you thought of. When you get there it will be the present and things may be very different than back then when you made all you're plans. Either in situations, the place or time we live in, or in yourself and others. So yes make plans but realize that. Don't live in the present only for a future that might never be and even if it does you might find it's not as it seemed or as you want or wanted. The only place you will ever truly exist is in the present that is where you should be because it exists and it is real. And it's the only time in your life when you can do something for yourself or others. And you can change or do things to try and make it happen. And even if it doesn't you at that time it is happening can do something about it, or deal with it, now in the present.

You can look at you're past maybe to learn good and bad from it. But don't exist there, you can't. Look to the future and what you'd like for yourself. But don't try to exist there again you can't. Open yourself to the present because one day it will be you're past and it will again affect your present and that affects your future. It may sound confusing it's not. And it's true.

LIVE, EXIST IN THE HERE AND NOW, THE PRESENT. You're in it and it out of the three is the only one you can do anything about good or bad for yourself or others. So live today, it's the only day that you or I will live in, after all it is the present, and its NOW.

## Momentary Fool

Sometimes people are scared to say what they feel or believe with people. Sometimes because they think they will look silly or foolish. There is a saying, try to believe and understand it because it's true. You know you don't want to look back one day and think, I wonder how things would have turned out if, I would have said or done something I know I wanted to or should have. "It is better to be a fool for a moment in time, than to live a lifetime as one" so say it. Things might be as you want. And yes they may not be. But if you don't ask, say or do something you may never know. And that is truly foolish but don't worry we all do it at one time or another. But things will be better if you bear this in mind. You will always have more to gain than lose if you think about it. Like the truth one way or another. It's far better to base, what you say, do, think or feel on the way it is. So be a momentary fool at worst and a lifetime not as one at best.

## The Message

When you hear things from others, that *are* bad, I know it is hard but please try not to take it deep into your heart and mind because it will corrupt you, damage you, hurt you. As if you read these things I write. It is not for you to feel sad. But that some good may come of it. Some of it may help you as it has helped me, or to understand the way you feel if it is bad. And understand that, until you know this you can't really tackle it. It is no different than the physical. Before a doctor can help you, he must diagnose you and the problem. THE HEART AND MIND IS NO DIFFERENT.

17

# The Bridge (Temptation or Realization)

That bridge does not exist. It is not a dark place it is a light. It shines brighter than anything, it gives off more heat and warmth than anything, it is more powerful than anything. It is in me as it is in all of us whether you know and believe it. It is there none the less. I hope and pray when you need it. It will show itself to you. Or you realize it is there so it can save you as it did me. What is it? The core of you, the deepest core of you, good, bad, special or not it is there. I'd love to let it shine in you and me always. So that when you need it, it will definitely be there for you, a Bridge? I cannot jump from it no more than you can push me off of it. There is no bridge for me no more. ONLY THAT LIGHT

# The School of Life

True knowledge that can only come from life
You see life is my teacher, life is my school
I never have to worry about being on time
Homework that is that I try extra
To learn to enhance life for myself and others
My detention is the mistakes I make
And the consequences that come with them
This teacher shows me good and bad
This school I will always attend until the end
When I leave this school I will leave this life
And then I will find out for real the true meaning
Hey maybe there is a next stage, college or
University in some other existence
Anyway I must go I hear the bell
The bell for the start of my next lesson
In life

**A DIARY EXTRACT...** Sunday night I went up to casualty. I did this because I can't bring myself to go to my doctors at the moment. I felt sorry for the doctor I saw, I knew she felt useless to help and she was concerned. It was nice to see her concern that at least I know it really does exist for me, from at least one doctor. But the ones who want to help cant, and the ones that can, Wont. You know if they read all this I know what sort of conclusions they would come to, probably the same as the ones before. And most of them are so wrong. The truth can depress you sometimes. That in itself doesn't mean you are Psychotically Depressed, that's nonsense. You know there are something's you can't think of and be happy at that moment that it happened, or that it happens at all. Not if you are a loving caring person.

\*\*\*

Being creative isn't about trying, it's about doing. I've found if I force myself to try to write a song, poem and so on. It's never as good, because it's false and made. Where as if it flows straight out it's from within and it has true meaning and is truly creative. So don't sit and ponder and do. Let it flow, no matter what happens, that is when you are truly creative.

## Emotional Baggage

Don't live your life by what other people think and feel
Live it by what you know and want
Otherwise it will be someone else's life your be living
And not your own

19

# Enter into His Gates with Praise or Don't Enter

Love and true guidance are my only weapons but they are pure of heart, and will never fail me or you. There is no win or lose just who you are. Those gates are not Religious ones. They are the gates to life. ASK YOURSELF THIS. Do you want to endure it as you enter and go through? Or enjoy that when you can for yourself and others. You choose more to open or close that gate on yourself. And also what you do when you have made your choice. Open and enjoy is the only conclusion for true fulfilment either for yourself and others, there is really no other choice. I wish you well when you open that gate and go through. I have sorrow for you until you make that choice, for you will not see the good that life can be. Only the bad that is, sometimes. But you will see and believe always. Sadness is where you lie. But you are not far from fulfilment just a step. A step you must choose to make for you to get there. Believe me it is truly there for me… you… us. I know it is, because I've seen it, and I've been there.

***

THE HARDEST THING YOU WILL FIGHT WITH IS YOURSELF

***

THERE ARE MANY PATHS RIGHT AND WRONG<br/>ONLY THE RIGHT PATHS WILL TAKE YOU TO YOUR TRUE DESTINY<br/>THE WRONG ONES WILL ONLY LEAD YOU TO YOUR DESTINATION

***

Oh tell you how I feel or what I think? Ain't no one that's gonna like it. What's the point in caring? Caring is what fucks you up. But if you didn't, would you be any better than THEM?

## Love and Care, Pain and Hurt

Love and care can be the sharpest, most pointy knife you can point at anyone. It can cut more deeply and hurt more than physical pain ever could. That pain lasts longer and when the wound is reopened can feel the same or worse than when it first entered you. And after a while of happening, it becomes normal to you. It can eat you up inside until you find it hard to have normal feelings towards people. And then when people even say they care or love you. You can't accept it because of what it represents to you. And that breeds and gives you more pain. And you need love and care to at least co-exist with that pain and hurt. Or even one day replace it. For long periods of time that deep pain and hurt is there it changes your actions and you don't even realize it, at the time. You might not feel it for a while. And something happens in your life and you realize it and you once again feel it. And you thought it had gone.

They say "time heals all wounds" maybe that's true, it doesn't feel like it. Some wounds are so deep they can improve but will always be there, and even if it is true, how long? How long is this time, this pain to last? Like everything it can be a vicious circle, it's like it's a monster inside you that desires hurt and pain and when it happens it eats and grows. And it will always exist as long as you or others feed it. So I suppose it is in all of us. It's not that you can ever totally get rid of it. It's how big you let it become. The other side is, desiring love and care. That one must be fed. It needs to be bigger than the other one. Then happiness maybe can finally come to you, once again. Pain and hurt will always enter you in your life. But let love and care enter it too, it can not only soothe the pain and hurt. It can also make it worthwhile. Time does not heal those wounds... Love does, for you and others.

\*\*\*

WORDS ARE MEANINGLESS UNLESS THEY COME FROM WITHIN
ONLY IN ONES SELF CAN YOU FIND TRUE MEANING

21

# Life's Judges

At the time something is done by anyone of us. The difference between a good person and a bad person can be that when things happen, afterwards a good person feels guilty, a bad person doesn't. A good person tries not to even though they may fail, a bad person doesn't. You see the deed maybe the same in both cases and you may judge that person either way. But you may be wrong unless you know whether they tried not to or cared afterwards. Don't believe only a good person doesn't or a bad person does. We are all fallible and make mistakes it's not an excuse. If you don't you will judge people wrongfully the action may well be wrong but a mistake or a wrong doing does not make someone bad to the core. Look at your life, are you saying you've never done wrong or made a mistake? I don't believe so; you'd be truly unique if you could say that.

I've seen people who judge people and you look at their life and see no better. By all means say they have done wrong. But to judge someone goes further. To do so you must be able to be pure, not just a good person can any of us say that truly? I'm talking about judging people not declaring in that instant when someone has done wrong. A song says "judge not before you judge yourself" it's true. It's the same as when a woman was going to be stoned by people. Jesus said "let he who has not sinned cast the first stone" guess what? No one could, not honestly. Do not persecute a person because of one deed or a bad mistake we all have done so sometime in our life. If you do so you are no better than the ones you judge. And the same song goes the same way it says "I know I'm not perfect that I don't care to be. So while you talk about me make sure your hands are clean" also "while you point your finger someone else is judging you" believe it. I've met people I bet you have standing in judgment of others, deluding themselves that they even have a right to. You see I've never met anyone who is perfect I've met people who think they are. Quote from a film "believing one's self to be perfect is the sign of a delusional mind" TRUE. It is not possible to be perfect not people, nor machine. Believing yourself to be, is delusional, trying to be is imperfection itself. Trying to be good for yourself and in so doing others is the best you can do.

What gets me is there are yes some terrible things that I can never accept. But even then, it is not judging them ABUSE of any kind is the one thing I can

22

never accept not once. But people are judging people for not crimes, which abuse is, but for things that can happen or be done by many of us. OK, you may say I will never do this or that. I now know and others do to, you can never be honest with anyone until you're honest with yourself. Most of us are not. You may one day, you may not. I am, I know there are things I try to make sure do not happen. But I am honest with myself to realize of what I am capable of doing in some situations whatever they may be. If I am not honest with myself it does not mean I will do, but in fooling myself it is more likely to happen. Most people have at one time thought something bad, not many haven't, be honest with yourself. It may help it not happen or not happen regularly. You will be better off and so will others. Be honest with yourself to be honest with people. When you make mistakes learn from them so good may come from it.

On the road of life, there are countless choices, being honest with yourself might help you make the right ones. Those that sit in judgment on others always, they are on a roundabout and will never be on the real road of life until they stop. They will not stop your journey in life only their own. If everyone judged themselves first, you, me, all of us would be better off. Right and wrong is. You need not judge to know that. One day you may be at peace with yourself if you have not sat in judgment of us. Or maybe for all the judging you did near the end of your journey. You may finally judge yourself and realize in so doing, YOU were wrong. And your last judgment is on yourself, and that's the one that hurts... YOUR LIFE HAS JUDGED YOU. Not us.

The Previous Poems were what I wrote in the Journal *before* I had it confirmed that I had been abused in Childhood. Significantly you can see more positive writing and descriptions of how I felt, trying to record and make sense of it all for myself.

The Poems **"Door to Life"** and **"Yourself"** to me help express the struggle deep within of, who and what you are, and where you've been. But this I still didn't know and so that's where looking back now afterwards it starts to make sense to me exactly why I was writing these things. They all now build the picture of the consequences of abuse and trauma. I was lost in life but also worse still, I couldn't find me, who I was. If indeed I really ever had been anyone.

**"The Pond of Life"** was my journey back, until it ended and had to be restarted. I was trying to work out my place, our place in the scheme of things. And just wanting to be without the struggle life can be.

**"Onwards and Upwards"** tells of the realization of the very long struggle ahead. And for every move forward you make the frightening awareness of the risk and how quick and far you can slip back.

**"Mankind's True Legacy (part one)"** is trying to show that being a realist and seeing the bad that *is* in this world, doesn't in itself warrant the label Psychotic depressive, or any other like it. I wasn't down at the beginning but when the enormity if it all hit me. I was down and naturally so. Next thing, it's not that they (Drs) then said I was depressed. It was Psychotic Depression. Which the only answer for was drugs? This made me feel worse. It's like the diagnosis is... it's you, but... they have a drug for that. I became even more lost. At the end it talks of "to deny a problem is to never solve it". It's certainly a step that no matter what others do, it's true. And you won't do a great deal until you take that step. But please let me add. That's not an excuse for anyone to say, they can't do anything until you do, because that's not true. At any time when you're vulnerable someone just being there, is never to be underestimated. Ask the Samaritans.

**"You Are Me"** a glimpse of love within? That's for you to decide.

24

**"Past, Present and Future"** I just want to say that quite a lot of this stuff is where I was on my own. At one point (not sure when) I found myself, self counselling. And I'm sorry, doing a better job than those qualified too, truth not bitching. This shows this, but I ain't going to tell you that I have done what's in this piece, fully. But at some point whether you like it or not (and I don't) you have to. That's the way it is. I just hope like me one day you will be ready and maybe we can meet on the other side. I'm not there yet. But I know it is important to see all that is contained within this piece. Adding also, it is not right for this particular stuff to be forced, or preached AT you. A lot of this is a personal journey. And yes some have done, some are ready, some are not but for me most importantly some never sadly will be ready, maybe that will be me, but if it is me, you. Let's not be blamed yet again for the way things are that we never chose. We live with it. That's enough.

**"The Bridge"** I wrote because of two things. First at the end of 2002, I had built up my hope. An appointment with a Psychiatrist took away my hope. You cannot live without hope. If I didn't know this before I knew on that day and the days that followed. The day started out so good. I would stand my ground with him, and question him and his care, as he discharged me from their... care? I left deeply upset, hurt. I walked across a bridge in a slight daze. I stood looking over and down. So knocked back I found myself saying "why don't I do myself and everyone a favour, and just jump" It scared me I moved away and went home. For a few days I was scared to go out. Scared of what I was feeling. I believe this was the most prominent thing that began over the next four months to unlock some truth not just of my childhood but of the recent past, and the present too.

The second thing was, I was so low you could not be, any more lower and be alive. I was on my bed I barely went out of my room let alone the house. Slumped across my bed, trying to starve myself (self harm) hating myself if I so much as eat a biscuit, telling myself "if you want to die, why are you eating?" Punishing myself, believing others wanted me dead. No one cared. I slump there so so low. So down, and yes I was depressed. I couldn't take much more. Scared I slump there feeling all this as something happened that I will never forget. Suddenly I started to feel this feeling I can only describe, as a warm glow inside. It was so beautiful the difference between that and what I had just been feeling was so opposite. I felt tearful. This feeling didn't last long. But I was so glad to have experienced it, at least once. I remember getting up and saying "that you all want me dead is why I will live. To be a constant thorn in your side" I know it might sound negative. But I didn't just get up there and then but for some time to come. But what made me write this? Well a friend of mine, a good one at the time. He knew nothing about any of it. Believing it was over and that I had turned a corner and that it wouldn't happen again. I told him. He was obviously concerned. So I wrote "The Bridge" to show to him, to put his mind at rest, which did help. But it wasn't the last time I felt this desperate. But I am still here. And at least something inside me fights it. With that light, that love, whatever it is. Just be glad it's there.

**"The Bridge"** is obviously very significant. The bridge incident happened in September 2002. As the previous description of it says. This led to months of realization, contemplation and an awakening of the truth. But again a general truth of people around me and the inappropriate ways I had been treated, in adulthood, but still not about my childhood. I began to see that these people I'd been around all my life were not in the way I had projected them within myself to be. Though as now I still loved them which only ever made it all worse. My Mum was almost the last one I could believe in that I loved and, loved me. This sadly began to waver as the truth began to escape.

The next few months were painful and I had some difficult experiences. Christmas time and winter time is always difficult, but that year even more so. But I got through it and began to rebuild and try again, but in January 2003 this came crashing down when I had severe flashbacks, but not of my childhood this was of things that happened in my teens. And in dealing with this as best I could, without exposing other truths about other things which would hurt those involved. I sadly had it confirmed I had been Abused in childhood, and something I had in my head was real and it was a Flashback, The one about being sexually abused by my Dads workmate. Of which I must say some within the Health Service would even have the nerve to blame me, the adult for later in life. Oh if only others could see. **"Questionable Anger"** and its introduction will pick up on this again later.

**"The School of Life"** I think this is a hopeful Poem and trying to be positive of the scheme of things including our or life's purpose. It's certainly not all doom and gloom that's for sure.

**"A Diary Extract"** this is the only one like this in here. But I thought it was important to help build a fuller picture of things, and understand what was going on, in and around me. And that it wasn't just me against the system or Dr's for instance. I mean I truly felt sorry for this Lady Dr. She cared and wanted to help. And in the end I had to tell her not to worry and that everything was going to be alright. I was consoling her.

**"Emotional Baggage"** one day I realized that's how I had lived a lot of my life. That made it not my life and not a life to live. Don't make the same mistake, but if you do... change it. It's your life, not theirs.

**"Love and Care, Pain and Hurt"** This deals with the consequences of abuse and neglect but also, it's making sense of it all and has a plan. For you know what needs to happen. You need more of the other side, Love and Care. So that when you do feel, it's not just pain, or always seeming that way.

**"Life's Judges"** is all about those sitting in judgement on us, all the time. Let's just let it stop their journey and not ours. I don't need to add to that.

This next Part starts with the direct aftermath of having it confirmed that I'd been abused in childhood. This happened in January 2003, with all the realization and its consequences that were about to follow. What made it worse, as always, I'd really been trying and achieved a lot and was looking forward positively. To then yet again have something out of my control undo it all. Cruel is what it was. But that doesn't change it. It happened and this is what came out of me after. And when you turn these pages and see what I wrote, I hope this can then make sense of it all. Remembering I was for the most part alone. And although I had two friends around me at the time, it all would become too much and our friendship in time would sadly end. That I understand from all sides. And I was also still not getting the right help and support from the Health Service.

In the direct aftermath, the overriding feeling was that my whole life and world was based on a lie. It fundamentally blew me away. And everything I knew was gone. It wasn't real. It wasn't true. I remember looking around at people I'd known all my life and I didn't know who they were anymore and worst, didn't know if I wanted to. And I didn't feel that much different about myself. You can see that in the things I wrote before. So as you can imagine my mood wasn't about to get any better. And as I've said, I was struggling mentally before, so that got worse. I could barely cope with just being. I had to leave home at first staying in my van my state of mind was rocky (naturally) and I was so vulnerable. For a few months, with a friends help I got into a hostel which was actually new and the people were nice. But my health issues got in the way. I couldn't eat there and with other people around me, at that time I couldn't handle it and in the end I had to leave and stay in my van again. I eventually got my flat, just in the nick of time. It was all spiralling out of control. I will go into more detail after this next part of the book.

Note. These next sections do contain *some* strong language.

## Best to...

Don't like men, don't like women. Children are alright they are pure but they will unfortunately become men and women and carry on the cycle of pure then impure. Don't like yourself. People and their love and care be aware it's only a matter of time before it is painful and it hurts. Caring is what fucks you up. And if like me, you cared more than others, it just then hurts you more and is more painful. Other species are alright at least unlike us you know where you stand. Not right? Then I don't know what world you live in, but it ain't the one I've seen and known.

\*\*\*

Death is a release
Life is terminal
You don't agree?
I don't know what
World you live in
I know the one
I believe in
It does not exist
And never will

## Abuse

WHY? Is the answer
To the question
That there can never
Be no reason

# Thanks to You

Back here again
This is no end
This is to begin
Once again

Sad I feel
I know it is real
That's the difference
That I feel

Life is out there
And so will I be
That I swear

This is to
Those that care
I'll be out there
And we can share

So watch out
And be aware
I'll be back
No doubt about that
It's a fact

Thanks to you
And the good you do
From me to you
I THANK YOU

With love from
Your friend John

*This was written while in Hospital, my second stay. It was to thank my friends. I had hope and I wanted to show it.*

30

# The Dream of Life

I am a failure because I try
I'm sad because I care
I'm a fool because I want to believe
Its my fault because I keep...
Trying, Caring, Believing
Even as it destroys me inside
And those near me
What makes it worse is
It might even be possible
A dream that could be
But never will
To do so you need people
And its people and their ways
That make it not possible
They create what's inside
Then blame you for it
Till you become what they say
So they can destroy you more
Till you have no fight left
Not even for yourself
To try is to destroy the dream...
Of life

\*\*\*

"THE DREAM OF LIFE" IS ALWAYS THE ONLY WAY IT HAPPENS
WHEN I think it, see it in my head as a boy, young lad to adulthood and the
moments I've tried in the flesh they stop it. So I dream of a life and what I
want, again with the knowledge it can never happen for the people and their
systems won't let it happen for me. That's the reality, it is not an illness these
words are real and not just how I feel.

TO GAIN WISDOM, FIRST YOU MUST LISTEN
TO RECEIVE ENLIGHTENMENT, YOU MUST BE READY

\*\*\*

They say there's a thin line between genius and madness. There's a thinner one, between life and death.

\*\*\*

When things make sense
You don't only need help
You're beyond it

\*\*\*

LIFE IS CHEAP. BUT IT COST ME A LOT

*Told a councillor that's what I'd have on my Gravestone*

\*\*\*

Respect is like love and most things in life
It's a two way street
And if you ain't coming down it
You won't see me

MEN ARE C\*\*TS
WOMEN ARE BITCHES
AND I AM NOTHING

\*\*\*

I only exist when they want to hurt me. Truth, reality, dreader than the world we live in.

\*\*\*

BEWARE
OF THE
~~DOG~~
WORLD

\*\*\*

Ain't no meek that inherit the earth
It's the filth and they are everywhere

\*\*\*

Denial of the world is what keeps me alive
Reality and truth is what kills me

*Some of the things above I wrote on a board that was in the back window of my van. Blocking it out when I was staying in it.*

# Why?

Being good, innocent and right not only is it no protection it is why it will happen to you because those things are what makes you vulnerable. It's sad being what you are or what you were makes you week. And when those things happen it turns those things upside down. Changes you inside and you become what you never were or never would have wanted. And it has destroyed something precious and something you can never truly get back. The wrong can never be righted. You can never do "the accept", cope or deal or the others. They may say learn to live with it, all of it. You can't, you either live with it or you don't. Either way it has destroyed part of you no matter what they say.

# People and Their Care and Help

They are all the same, People, friends, family, all people, all the same. They give up on you straight away if they even try, or not long. Then what's worse, they hurt you more. You're already going out of your mind. They don't care they do all they can to make it worse. How much more can you take? not much more, you're on your own again as you have always been. You live longer that way, so do others. And they all stand around ignore or watch your perpetual torment and torture. They say tell them when you do, they punish or persecute you for it. Doctors have been the same my life to them is not worth saving if they give any help it fucks me up, they fill me with their bullshit. That fucks me up. Little that I ask, so I can again, try to live, what I long for. But they all stand in my way every time I try. I have a thought or two about the things life could be, it just makes me feel like crying they won't let it be possible. "GOD!" I said the other day "why don't you just kill me?" I can't take it to tackle one thing let alone all of it. They tell me they care or they will help as they draw that weapon to hurt me some more. Go away? Where shall I go? I'm already dead inside. Maybe I'm just waiting to die.

# Loving Flower

They always make excuses. "He hits me but he loves me" or "it's my fault I upset him" NO it's because he is a worthless piece of shit. And you are a flower. And he's jumping up and down on that flower. Though you may still look like that flower. The crushed petals at his feet are what you feel inside. If you cared enough about yourself, you would see. They call it domestic violence, there is nothing domesticated about it. Take the word domestic away and what do you have? VIOLENCE Otherwise known as ABUSE, of which like all of us you don't deserve. No one does. I wish you could see the flower that I see and the crushed petals at his feet that you sometimes don't see, but feel. But you need to see and know it to be what you are, that loving flower, a flower that needs love, and deserves it too.

# Who and What Am I?

When you know you look at me different. You would not be normal if you didn't. But remember I am the person you knew yesterday before you knew all of this. Today you know what I am, yesterday it was who I am. If you can't see who I am, only what I am, then we can never be the same together in anyway. I am not what you hear, not what you know, I am what you see and feel. That is who I am to you. Not what I am to you.

\*\*\*

YOU CAN LOSE A LOT ON ANY JOURNEY
WHO OR WHAT YOU ARE... THAT'S A LOT
THAT'S SOME JOURNEY

# Where Am I?

It is dark here
I am on my own
It is longer than wide
But wider than high
If there is another
You are higher now
Yet you are low down
In reality
You're only represented by words
People may pass you
They will not see you
No matter how near
Or how far
The sun may shine
You will not see it
Rain may fall
It will not touch you
The wind may blow
You will not feel it
Do you know yet?

Almost all of you
Will be here
Here's the biggest clue
The words that represent you
Are in or on stone
Like the Ten Commandments
Six feet down
Flowers maybe placed
Above you?
Surely now?
Yes?
I am in my grave

# The Game

It's a good game you're all playing
You're all going to get what you want
No matter what I do
The problem is, I'm not a participant
I am the game
Play well for you can never lose
The game is not with me
It is me
It must be good to play
Knowing you will always win
don't worry
Me... my life... it is the game
I congratulate you all
It's a game everyone
Seems to know and play so well
I await you or their next turn
The next throw of the dice
To see what it may bring for me next
A game like any other
Winners and losers
They must be mindful of this game
As with all games it will end
But there are always other games
Now before and in the future
Some play and don't even know it
But the dice is thrown none the less
Some know and enjoy
I live in the knowledge
Life is no game
Those that treat it like one
I have no time for
But the players are always there
Everywhere you go
So play the game
Play it well
But hope that you will always be a player
And not the game itself
Like me, like us
The game

# Writer?

No I am not a writer. I don't like labels. I look at it this way. There is a lot more to life than that that which can be explained. I pray for the day it shall never be. It could undo it and it wouldn't be the same. Words come in my head I now as I used to put pen to paper and it flows out. Whenever I tried to do it, it was crap. It like all good things comes from the core within. My body is a vessel, my hands are the instrument and this pen and paper are the tools. How good is it? Well that's not relevant. Has it touched you without physical touch? If it has, then the good is inside you.

# Writer Part Two

You see I learned to read and write. I did not learn to write poems, songs or philosophy. It is not something I learned. It was there. How? Why? There are many reasons known and unknown. I did not make it. How could I? We should not reason why. Just be thankful. I have sometimes truly experienced this, when it comes from within, through you reading it verbally to someone. And sometimes you know it has touched them deeply. And you smile, because you know it has. That's the gift and the power of the word.

*Dedicated to Bill the one Councillor who made such a difference and seemed to hear when I spoke. Something I will never forget. But sadly when he left it all went downhill for me.*

In all the years
In all that's been done
That we both know
Can't be undone
You took time, to believe
To undo what you see
No job, no money
Does this believe me
Only the good inside
That I see
That you can
That you might
Is not the thing
That you did and do
Is what you bring
So don't forget
What you have done
So you can bring it to
ANOTHER ONE

# Game on

Ok I'm playing the game. Let's get it on. I'm not playing the game to win. I ain't that stupid enough to think I can. I'm playing to lose. Let's get this fucking game over with. You think it matters? You think it amounts to anything, the pinprick in the ocean? YOU sad bastards, what can you do that ain't been done? You've been in the cue too long. It's gone to your head. You're too late. Ain't nothing much left, not enough to satisfy you if you only knew. I, as always am destroying what's left, it's a kindness that I do to myself. Unlike those that say they care. They can't see there's a kinder and better way. And to you that play, we want the same thing game on my friend. You would stop if you knew and truly understood. Your winning is my winning, and your loss is mine. So play me like a fiddle my friend, it only proves one thing. You're sadder than me and that's saying something. Why hate? when I can pity you, you sad bastards.

From

The Game That Plays

# Sometimes

Wanting is better than having
Fantasizing is better than doing
Not knowing is better than knowing
Not believing is better than to believe
Not seeing is better than seeing
Not hearing is better than hearing
Blissful ignorance rather than reality
Untruth rather than the truth

# Is it a Game like Chess?

You know the game it can be like chess. Sometimes you realize you can't win. So all you can then do is try and get it to stalemate. When that happens no one wins. But it's the best you can do. So you don't beat them but you make sure they can't win. How it affects them depends on how much winning means to them. But if stalemate happens you are on top because you couldn't have won anyway. But they could have. You got the best you could have. But they lost, because unlike you they played with the chance of winning. It's a chance I lost a long time ago. Just things re-enforce that over the years. Stalemate is absolute to you but not so for them. There is another way which I found just making the game continue. That gets too much. And unlike stalemate cannot end without total loss. You just prolong the inevitable. In so doing are you not playing their kind of game anyway? All these pieces, I've lost the understanding of how they even move. It would not be so bad but they seem to know all the moves. I am cleverer than they think but their pieces, their pawns, their rooks, they're always protected. Yours are not they after every move are more vulnerable than you could ever imagine. Would you choose not to move any of your pieces? Sooner or later you have to. They are in the knowledge of this. And they await your move they pre-empt it sometimes. Is it a game like chess? In one way it is not. In many ways it is. The one reason it is not is that in chess you are a player in real terms. But in this game you are more like a pawn, because you are the game. I grow tired deep within of this game. Once I even believed I could be a player. But after many of their moves they unlocked the real game to me. It wasn't a fair move. For you are only supposed to move one at a time in sequence with each other. They did not. They moved countless times more than I could count or know. In the time it takes to make one move. And I know they are going to do it again, whether I move or not. They are many players. Do you not think that it's a bit one sided? But hey it's just a game after all… isn't it? I stop now. I don't want to move. They move none the less. One day we shall see how it all unfolds, like now, like then... Who cares? Playing the game is the only thing that really matters to them. But it isn't chess.

# A Moment

As I wrote in "Past, Present and Future" its O.K. to focus on the future but don't forget to live a bit today. As someone once said about "rather living for a moment as a freeman than a lifetime as a slave", I as he was. I'm a moment because really that's all any of us are, a moment in time. So live that moment as its happening and if possible enjoy it so you can truly live it. When they say "live for the moment" say "no I am that moment" for good bad happy or sad, as life's rocky road is. So have the moment you and all of us are. Even when it's bad, so that you can live through to the moment of good, that most of us deserve. How long or close it is to you me or any of us? We just have to wait and see like all truly good things it cannot be made or fabricated. It just is or isn't. GOOD LUCK FOR YOUR MOMENT.

# Side Affect

They wouldn't know care if it kicked them up the arse
Life's a side effect of being born
Near death is when the side affect is wearing off
Death is when it has

# The Risk of Happiness

You must make yourself open to someone otherwise you cannot be truly happy. But to do so you become vulnerable to the other side, pain and hurt. But to shut yourself off to someone to deny a chance of being hurt you also in so doing, shut yourself off from the good and happiness. The good side carries a risk as all things but without the risk of the pain, happiness and joy cannot come. If you have a chance of happiness, it is a risk worth taking but you will not truly know this until you try. But without that risk it will never come anyway. The choice like the risk is yours.

# The Price

Doesn't take long for normality of which you know to be, and for people and life, to show its true colours to you again. It's a sadness you cannot escape from. For it just continuously happens. And that you notice it. You are made to feel bad or even persecuted for. The crime is noticing and knowing the truth, that which they wish to deny, that which they wish not to accept. It would interfere with their lives, their answers, their conclusions, their reasoning, their lies. So even though it destroys somebody else or worse, it's a price they think is worth paying. But it is you who pay the price not them. A price that is not and never will be worth paying. It's easy to think it's a price worth paying… when it's not you that will pay the price.

# Not This Journey

You know I'm on a journey there's plenty of room for people. But I don't want to take people I don't like with me, let alone people I like. But they keep on coming. It seems like they want to come to. As I say to them whether I like them or not. NO for where I'm going there is no return.  I may not want to be on this journey but I certainly don't want to take anyone with me. But they still try so. It's ironic I am reluctantly on this journey. They want to so much. But I know the destination. Yet they don't seem to. For if they did when I am on this journey. They certainly wouldn't want to journey with me.

\*\*\*

MY PRINCESS HAS THE KEY, NOT JUST TO MY DOOR
BUT TO MY HEART AS WELL

## The Juggling Drs

They're juggling balls
Those balls
Are human lives
They have in their hands
Occasionally they drop one
That is not the worst
That they don't bother
To pick it up
IS
As another is thrown
In its place
They continue as though
Nothing has happened
Unfortunately
The ball that dropped
Was a human life
That they did not even try
To pick it up
Is why it's gone
Not a ball
A human life
Is a life not worth more?
I BELIEVE IT IS

# Britons in a Spin

Three for the cost of one?
Not for the price of
New Labour
New Briton
Old Conservatives
Spreading the pain
Liberally
Oh we can see you change
Others do not feel it
Cause it feels the same
The problems still the same
Is there any wonder?
With these three
Costing us the ones
Is there really a choice
Between them?
In this Briton
The Land we Love
That's in a Spin
That you did begin

# Lifer

My crime was being born
For which they punish me for
Yet it is the one thing
I cannot feel guilty about
It could not be my fault
Being born was not my choice
I obviously was not here
When that choice was made
Yet they punish you for it
Just like everything else
That they do
We are punished
For their crimes and sins
We carry theirs
Along with ours
That's what our lives are
To carry what they should
To be blamed for their doings
That's Life
A real Life Sentence

# The World of Silence and the Silence You Shame

The world is full of abusers
The minority are here to be abused by you
Mustn't disobey
Mustn't tell
Or you will be abused by others
In the name of
Love, care, help or treatment
It's not the real abusers
That create the worse reasons to be silent
It's you and what you do
That creates the world of shame and silence
I must be ready
I have spoken out
Even in words
When they read this
They will come and abuse me again
Maybe it's my fault after all
Maybe you're right and I'm wrong
That's a shame
or
Is it shame?
You decide
Shall I be silent?...
Like before

## Up the Real Creek

They may find
At one time like me
You're up shit creek
Without a paddle
But worse than that
You ain't even
Got a boat
And if anything
Like mine
Swimming in my shit
Just ain't possible
Let's face it
You really are
Up the creek
You better hope
Someone drags you out
Before you drown
In your own shit
YOUR REAL
Shit creek

# Johns Gone

Johns gone
He ain't coming back
I'm new
My names John
You don't know me
You never will
Just like the other John
The one that's gone
NOT this John
Don't worry
It is confusing
There are so many Johns
That have been and gone
Maybe I'm like…
The other Johns
And it won't be long
Before I'm gone
You know
John
By the way
What's your name?
It's not…
John is it?


B y-e- J o h n

## BASED ON THE EXPERIENCES OF MYSELF AND OTHERS

## C.M.H.T.

Community? There isn't one. Yes we all wish there was

Mental? They certainly are i.e. some of their staff

Health? That's a joke. That doesn't improve

Team? They're a team when they want to fuck you like they did me

Community like care in the community is based on something that doesn't exist anymore, even the sense of it. Ask most people. Mental some of them are more delusional than the patients. Health it can deteriorate through them. It is wrong. Team not with or for you but can be used against you. I know we don't live in an ideal world. But while these things are or can be true to the most vulnerable in our society, if that exists for the benefit of all. Then we will never even come close. The way to judge society is not to look at all the well off or the top. But to look at what happens to the ones at the bottom, how they are helped and treated. I wish I could say something different but like others who spare a moment to think about it. I am ashamed. For if this is a so called civilized society. The word has new meaning to me, because it's not so civilized to some I have known and see. It doesn't ring true of the definition of the word that I learnt.

## Given Too Much

I know I'm a nightmare
But I do try
I wouldn't be here if I didn't
But they try…
They try my patience at best
They give me a choice
You know… no choice
I suppose it's a choice
Not one you make
One given to you
Like everything else
I wish they stopped…
Giving to me
I can't afford it anymore
They've already given me…
Oh so much
Thanks a lot
No I mean that
But there must be…
Someone more deserving than me
Please give to them
I'm sorry to sound so ungrateful
But you've already
Giving me too much

# The Reflection in the Mirror

Just like when you look in the mirror
It has a reflection of you
What you do to others has one
It reflects back at you
As good as a mirror
It is a reflection of your attitude
Towards others
So be careful what you do to others
Just like when you look in that mirror
You can't hide from your reflection
As with you can't hide
From what you have done
You may get a reflection back
That you don't like
The world is a mirror
It reflects on what you do
Hopefully you will be able
To look at yourself
And like what you see
When it reflects back on you
A picture can lie
THE MIRROR DOESN'T

# Our Silence

We speak but you refuse to hear
We speak but you won't believe
We speak but you won't understand
A silence that drowns out words
A silence that drowns out a cry
I try not to hate you but pity you
The silence you shame is yours not ours
Because there isn't really a silence is there?
It's what you create that we learn to hate
But it's all around because it's in us
It pops up when you don't want it to
Because the silence doesn't make up for the fact
That we know and you know that we do
Even though you're more silent than us
I'm afraid like ours your silence speaks volumes
Believe it or not we're in the same boat
But one of us was wronged, the other did wrong
Our silence is because we were wronged
But yours, is because you are wrong

# The Final Equality

It doesn't matter what you say you are. It doesn't matter what race or religion you are. It doesn't matter rich or poor. It doesn't matter how big you think you are. It doesn't matter what you have or haven't done. It doesn't matter whether you agree with it or not. Your age, sex, or class doesn't matter. For it is the same and equal for one and all. Embrace it or fear it. It does not matter. It is the most constant of all things, everlasting but equal for all. No matter whether you are the above or something else, but if only there could be equality in life that there is in death, for us all. Wouldn't that be something?

# The Wall that Confines You

You can build up a wall around yourself sometimes, to try and protect yourself from people and things. Acting like you don't care, when you do. Portray yourself to be the opposite of what you are as a defence and protection. But the problem is even unbeknown to someone because you care they don't need to get through the wall you have created to get at you. Just trigger it inside you, because you care. And when that happens you may find that wall not only doesn't protect you always. When that happens it becomes like a prison that confines you where you feel that pain and hurt on your own. Instead of protecting you it confines you. And can as a consequence stop those that do care about you from being able to help you. We must try to take down that wall. Otherwise that wall will only get bigger and thicker and taller. You know? - That wall of confinement not protection. It must come down to let out that you do care, so you can feel that we do and that's our protection. Not a wall, but the fact we do care about each other. That's our strength, that they don't is their weakness, always alone as they are. When we realize that we can help each other with our care. And let them create a wall that confines them. That will never protect them from the fact that unlike us they don't care. And that's why our wall will come down a lot easier than theirs ever will. Caring isn't a weakness though it hurts sometimes. That even then deep down we still care shows, a STRENGTH in us, NOT a weakness. Let it be OUR wall of strength that bonds us TOGETHER. Not a wall that keeps us apart. That only helps them hurt us and stops us FROM HELPING EACH OTHER.

\*\*\*

Make sure someone is with you for who you are, not what you are.

\*\*\*

The system has a funny way of protecting the perpetrators. Making victims of the innocent and punishing those who take the law into their own hands because of the above. Not always but too many times this rings true. It brings more meaning to the words, inadequate and failing.

# The Survivor

If you have survived a moment
Then you can survive another
If you have survived a day
Then you can survive another
If you have survived a week
Then you can survive another
If you have survived a month
Then you can survive another
If you have survived a year
Then you can survive another
You can survive
Because you already have
Because you are a survivor

That you hear or read these words
Is that you have survived
It might not get any easier
But that you are here now
Is testimony to the fact
That you are a survivor
Believe me I know like me
You can do this we can survive
Its not as unbelievable as you may feel
After all we already have and do
You me... we are not the survivor
We are the survivors
Because many are we

I hope like me you see
To make a survivor of **WE**
And not just me

# Facing Up

When you face up to the bad things, you can undo some of the damage as I said before "to deny a problem is to never solve it". We may not want to face up to it. But if we don't it will never change and that's something that we do to ourselves. Yes they may help it be that way. That's the one thing that we must know we control, whether we face up to it. And we must, for us not them. They may not want us to, but that's our choice to make. We must recognise that so we can help ourselves and not carry on what they have done or do. It's a hard choice but there really isn't another way. It just leads to our lie, in our denial, and when you realize this you know and feel it's even worse than theirs for what it does to me and you. And that's facing up to it. And it's hard. But it's the only way.

# Up or Down

I got this thing, if success means stepping on everyone, to climb the greasy pole of success. Whatever it is, it will never be enough or worth it to me. I need to be able to sleep at night. I sleep better in the gutter when that's the case. I am disturbed by many things but not my conscience. Which when you are decent is the most disturbing of all. The greasy pole of success may seem or even take you to the top. But in those cases, it is a downward slide from decency from within, and selfish. Success in itself is not selfish, how you get there can be. So remember as you climb the pole of success. Make sure that you really are going up, and not down.

# For You Louise

You had a smile that shone like the sun. And when it touched us it had warmth warmer than the sun itself. You were a ray of sunshine in the darkness. The years have not diminished that warmth, glow, and love. Though it is deep it comes to the surface again with thoughts and pictures of you, and the tears well up from within, from a love still strong that you gave to us. I am sorry I can't tell you in the flesh but within myself I only hope you can see, hear and feel it. That from within can never really lie, people are sometimes special but none more so than you. I feel sorry for myself I admit that I and maybe others did not appreciate you as much as we should have. For that I am sorry. But as all special ones you did not give to receive. Just hope like all of us that you would. What I feel now something tells me, and I hope that you know. When people I care about smile it makes me smile and lights up my heart. You did more than that Louise. When you smiled your smile lit up the room... our lives... and still does. And that's no lie or exaggeration. You seemed to lie in wait patiently to smile again and bring and give it to us deserving or not. What happens when we leave this life I like others, do not know for sure. But what I do know above all else is. If there is a good place not only are you there but you are the centre of it, as it should be. And in our lives darkness was not dark no more whether for a moment or longer when you smiled, it made the darkness go away. And as for the good place bright though it maybe it will always seem dim when your smile starts to glow. I don't need to say keep smiling. It's what you do. I say do because all these years and I can still see and feel your smile and always will. With love from someone, so lucky enough to have known, and been touched by you and your smile, Dearest Louise. I thank you.

From John and us all

You're just too good to be forgotten

# Surviving It, Us and Them

Alone truly I feel again, my fight is with the abusers, the ones doing it but sadly more so the ones belittling it, covering it up, making excuses while too many help them and deny us. They talk about it like you've just fell over and grazed your leg and you should just get up and carry on as if nothing has happened. The real fight, it's sad but it is with them that their attitude only helps the abusers to carry on, get away with it and give them all the excuses that they do anyway with or without them. Sometimes it's the fight that keeps you here alive to fight another day not physically, though you need the physical strength but mentally keeping it real not to lose a sense of reality and emotionally not to fall apart. You and me we need to survive sometimes it's a sad fact when I think, who will continue this fight if not us? Sometimes for ourselves we can see that we need personally to survive, for no one will carry the torch on our behalf if we are gone. And not enough within power in the right places at the right time.

We have power if we can harness it. Through the facts that are disturbing because they are true. As I said when I wrote "The Survivor" when I said "don't make a survivor of me make a survivor of we" I need you to survive, we need you to survive. If we do, out of one can come two then another from you. You from another and the same with me then we can make the people see. Out of one came two, out of two came four, and out of four came sixteen and so on. Until we are more than one and two, Maybe one hundred, maybe a thousand, maybe more. Then my voice and yours will and can be heard for as someone once said "out of many we are one", one voice, with enough to make it louder than theirs (the Abusers and their apologists). So that they have to listen, for they can no longer deny that they hear it. For others will know they do. I, you, we cannot change what has happened no matter what. And although I find it hard we alone cannot make it not happen to anyone else. I know for myself I cannot make it worth it. Nothing that is possible to happen can do that. But I believe if we survive, we can make a difference in a positive way.

For although I cannot make it worth it, I believe and know that I must do something to mean for myself that it is not all for nothing, and to do that to give a real meaning for my life and what has happened, it's the only thing that could consol me within myself, that at least something good and positive

58

can come out of it. I know I can't win because what I truly want will not happen. But what I do is, so that they don't win and in that at least I, we do not lose. And for all this and more, we first need to survive, I need you, you need me, we all need each other. Only if we survive can we make a difference to someone, people and each other. Our voice heard, it must make a difference how much depends but it is not really the point. Survive because we need to, do because we can, anything else only serves the bad people. I do everything I can, I will not go away, I am here and I will be a thorn in their side a reminder I am more than what they say, I am more than that what they did and do. I am more than a consequence of what they do, or a side effect. I, we are someone, we do matter, we are worthy, we did and do not deserve this, or these things.

I gather strength from you, born out of decency in people and myself. Whether I know you personally or not, I know you exist, I know you are there. You like me may feel alone but yet I know of you, I think you know of me. I am with you in spirit for all the good and positive you can do. If only for you to survive all this, I, we know for them that have a chance to speak on behalf of the abused, to do something about it and make a difference whether I do it, you or someone else that we don't personally know. We are in this together for each other for the sake of decency, love and the right. For the children or women or even men who are abused, but none more so than the children. We survive, take courage I know somewhere, somehow even if you don't. You have the strength. Out of one can come many. But out of many can come one, one voice, ours together. Just that you exist is testimony to everything you are and capable of doing. And a life you can have. Yes it will be hard but you deserve it. As much as anyone I know. Survive, do and then live. Because you can, you deserve it. And it's how it should be it's meant to be, now for you, me and we, TOGETHER.

***

Better to be rich in love, than be rich in money.

## Love Isn't the Lie

When the blade cuts your hand the words are irrelevant. When they use and abuse you the word counts for nothing. Someone once said to me "love is a big word" true or not, that's not the problem. It is that it is used more than is true by all of us. That's not so bad, as when it is used for abuse or rape of you and others, that word becomes a lie, meaningless. That they use it makes it so. But love is real and it exists within you, me and others. Love is not the lie. They are. Love isn't meaningless. Their use of the word is. It's their lie that isn't true. Not love. When you know and feel the one that counts. It's called love. And it's the one that's true and not a lie... unlike their words.

## Don't Deny Their Denial

Just because someone denies you you're basic fundamental human rights. Doesn't mean you don't have them. It means just what it says. They deny it. But you like all of us do have them. You must know that, or they will always win within you. It might not stop them denying you your rights. But do you want to help them? Let it be their denial. And believe me theirs is worse than ours. For theirs is dirty, unjust, abusive, all those things and much much more. It weighs our cross down heavy with a burden that is theirs. They don't carry it, but why should we?

SILENCE ISN'T GOLDEN
ISN'T SAFE
BUT IT'S SAFER

# The Ones

For I am one like you
We are the ones
Because sadly many are we
Together be strong know of us
Like you
To make a stronger one
In us all
Together not alone
For we know of each other
And how we feel
We know it is real
What we feel
Unlike some but remember
We are the ones
And we are in the know
Isn't that what makes things so?

# Leap Into Action after Death

Sometimes you find it hard to understand. About what these people will do if the worst happens and you die. Like all of a sudden their gonna leap into action and do what they couldn't, while you lived. Don't you think that's strange? Don't you think it's the wrong way around? Even if you believe they will. It's not easy to understand the way things are. Is it because I believe in an ideal world? Far from it, if you have a problem with the health service, a serious one. Then you're on your own mate. If you weren't before you are now. The organisations you may believe in, where are they?

# P. M.

We have waged war on terrorism. There has been the war on drugs. We've had zero tolerance. Is the day going to come when you publicly tell us of The war on the ABUSE of children? When you stand up as you have for the war on terrorism. The children of the world are not only our future THEY ARE THE FUTURE. If we lose the war for the children. We lose a future for a better world. Whether terrorism, drugs, abuse or any subject you could care to mention. Someone once said "he didn't see the sense in winning a battle to go on to lose the war." I believe that is what we are doing as a people as a society. Could you not publicly tell us "you wage war on the abuse of children"? And put the resources somewhere close to that which has been spent on the war on drugs or terrorism. Because all the other battles just as well be on the outside. There is something rotting at the core and the longer it is this way all the patching will not make a difference all the words or money will not. When the core the foundation to life itself THE CHILDREN has been eroded and overlooked compared to other policies home and abroad. We will only ever win battles but never win the war on behalf of JUSTICE, DECENCY and even HUMANITY itself. while the rights of the Abusers come before the rights of the Abused. ONLY THEY EVER WIN. While there is not enough of a network properly funded by government. It is more than we the abused slip through the net. The net was not there before during but worse still after. I speak from my experience and that which I have seen and heard of others. Until it is not mostly left to charitable organizations to fill a gap I believe the government this one and those before have left wide open and not filled. We the abused we the people we the lost children deserve better from the ones in power. I have met countless ones who battle to get counselling specifically for sexual abuse. And come up against disgusting attitudes and opinions from within the system and inept points of view. Only made bearable by the Samaritans and other well meaning caring people. Who unfortunately should have more power and money to do what they want because we know they would if they could. And not only what can be afforded. Compassion doesn't cost money, just the will to give it. Lack of help because of expense? I would say to them maybe we have cost the system but it will never come close to what it has, does and will cost us. Something of many things that no money can purchase. The lack of these things is what costs us all the most and society as a whole in ways that cannot ever be truly calculated but to know there is a cost for us all and it will not be just in the present but obviously in the future too. And if it is cost in money then more funding is needed. If it was given out of need then would we not have it automatically? The abusers didn't give up all their rights when they abused us. But they gave up a right to have rights that come before the right of the innocent those that have been abused and those that haven't. Yes they must be protected but not to the detriment of the vulnerable. And not to the detriment or risk to OUR basic human rights of protection from being abused or being abused again. The length of sentences of abusers is sickening. And it's a rape and abuse of us and society in itself. Justice? Confidentiality that only protects them? Unfortunately its worse too many times it serves them (oh too well). OUR rights are overlooked by them and others. It's time for OUR rights to come before theirs. THEY chose to Abuse THEIR RIGHTS **THEY HAD** when THEY ABUSED US. Don't let us pay for it again or worse still more children. The balance needs to be shifted the other way. So it can serve us (in the way it should) as well as it has served them (in a way it never should have). Controlling or overseeing is what they need. It is us the abused and the innocent that need protecting from them. Not them from us. Something some seem to forget in a way that WE NEVER WILL.

Yours sincerely

J R Harrison.


*The above letter has had the spelling corrected since it was first sent. More information about this letter you can see at the end of this book. It was sent April 2008.*

# Our Mother

I am an orphan
God is my farther
Earth is my mother
And I am her son
I hate God my farther
But I love my mother… earth
That from where I came from
That from what I was made
And there where I shall return
One day
And at that time I return
At the end to where I began
Returning to my mother… earth
Despite my father's doings
Sayings, proclamations, prophecies
Or even revelations not redemption
My mother earth
She is not contaminated
Not from within
Only around on the outside
Due to my father, us
And our doings
That what we have done to her
That is why I will always love her
My mother… earth
Blameless is she
And that she has given
For little or no return from us
Yet still she provides despite us
As best that way only she can
There is no better mother
Than our mother earth
And she is yours
Just as much as she is mine
So love our mother earth
Without her none of us would be

Or will be without her
Earth the mother of us all
And just like any mother
You only ever have the one
And there's no other like her
Now before or will be again
No matter what you believe
Religious or not
She spawned us all
From the very beginning
From the microscopic beginnings
Or from the soil that...
The farther began us all from
That still remains
This is our mother
Earth


\*\*\*


FOR WHAT YOU NOW WITNESS
I AM TRULY SORRY
DO NOT FEEL BAD DO NOT SHED A TEAR
FOR AS I LAY HERE IN THIS BATH
I HAVE FOUND AN INNER PEACE
I HAVE SEARCHED FOR ALL MY LIFE
THERE IS NO SORROW HERE
ONLY THAT PEACE

# My Saviour

Hate won't save your life
But it may take it
Bitterness won't help your life
But it might risk it
But Love can... save your life
Once... twice... many times...
For as long as it's there
And you can still feel it
Or it can still touch you
For as long as that's true
It can and will be your Saviour
Just like it's been mine

I'm just going to pick out some more of the Previous Poems and Prose to go into further, mention, or just make an important point from my point of you. But first as you can tell, it was hell and when I wrote, the truth came out of how desperately hurt, confused and overwhelmed I was. I'm afraid you may find it hard reading but it's the truth and there is genuine reason for it. And I believe if we all hide it then when someone feels these things it just doesn't help. We've got to know this is normal and I have done nothing wrong. I, to this day have no criminal record. I haven't hit anyone let alone anything else. And I want you, if you have been abused to see it's not unnatural or bad to think or feel these things. And for those who haven't been abused, maybe just maybe you might get a glimpse or even an understanding of what it can do to someone in the aftermath of finding out, and then trying to live with it? No more to the point, trying to survive the truth. I got to let people see it how it came out, naturally. If I change things it's not going to help. Nothing you are about to see previous or now is there to shock. No swearing, though there is a little, it's not there to offend, that's actually the last thing I want. As I want to engage with you. Not put you off. The first of the previous Poems and Prose expresses to you, all of that time, like...

**"Best to...", "Death is a Release", "Abuse" & "Men are C**Ts"** well this is where I was at. I just want to pick up on these first few to say, imagine you just found out. You can't comprehend it. I couldn't, and as others, it was happening to me, Painful to say the least. For me the fourth short but to the point said where my head was at, with myself and others around. But at least the anger and pain and all the rest I was expressing, was in a way that wasn't hurting anyone. And it was at least releasing some pressure. Not enough but some, through writing.

**"Thanks to you"** shows me being positive despite it all, written while trying to be seen properly by Drs and the CMHT in hospital. Trying to give my friends hope that I was going to get better and be back. We all believed this.

**"The Dream of Life"** this Poem left me seeing what I hadn't had and what I started to think I never would. But please this was based on what was and had actually happened. And it really was driven by the fact that every time I tried to move forward or get the right help I needed. Someone or something was in my way stopping me. And sadly it was usually Dr's.

**"People and their Care and Help"** as it sounds, desperate times, losing hope and the few people around me, I began to feel weren't on my side anymore. Extremely isolated and hurt and upset because I so wanted to live. And I was trying but again people were in my way stopping me from even having a chance.

**"Loving Flower"** So called Domestic Violence. This was written as a result of being around it. Who and the situation for this book actually doesn't matter, because like all Abuses, and that's what it is, there are similarities, Not least that you don't deserve it. And it's not acceptable. I remember standing as a fourteen, fifteen year old. Thinking that I was ashamed I was going to be a man. And if when I was older I ever felt like hitting a woman then it was time for me to go because no matter what it was she had done. It was obviously over. Shame others don't do that really. It deals with the reality even if you don't. You are someone. You don't deserve it.

**"Who and What Am I?", "You Can Lose A lot On a Journey..."** these describe the confusion of what's left when you have a block of your child hood and you become aware of your past. It shakes the foundations and when it does come out, you don't even know who you are, just what you are.

**"Where am I?"** This was at the point of living out of my van just before getting my flat. I was really vulnerable and deteriorating, I read it to a councillor, he knew of its significance. Luckily I got my flat and things improved for a while because I now had a foundation to build on.

**"The Game"** this just so sums up how I felt about my existence and how I had little chance as they had all the moves on me.

**"In All the Years that's been Done"** this was the message inside a card I gave to the one councillor I had, that made a difference in a profound way. Within months of knowing him, he, with me, turned things around. But sadly after not many months he had to leave. And my recovery and dealing with the sexual abuse ended there and then. But thank you bill, I will never forget the compassion you showed, and the help given to me by you.

**"Game On"** its rebelling against them. Let's get this over with, I've had enough. Or just leave me alone. And yes as you read it, it goes into and even is created through the anger. But a long time after someone heard it and it genuinely made us both laugh. Again that's the power of writing not just Poetry. It can turn that emotion around and can then be a Positive advantage.

**"The Price"** the main point in this is. It's that they, including people you love are willing to be silent even if it may take you to your grave. That's what hurts the most.

**"The Juggling Dr's"** this was not done out of spite or anger, this is about some of those people involved that call themselves Dr's (of any type). And it is what I was fighting against. And what I do now, trying to make sure that if people aren't going to do anything about it. At least I can tell people how it can be and expose it. It's the only way. True Accountability is so what we need.

**"Lifer"** Does anyone really believe that the system is giving Child Abusers long enough sentences? Maybe some, but for the most part, no its not and that (as I wrote to a Politician once) is one thing abusers are not to blame for. This Poem also expresses the life sentence we get, whether they do or not. All I want is for us to not be treated worse than them. And for them to face a proper sentence and one that's not an insult to us, children or society. Is that too much to ask? It seems so. But I will continue to ask for it. And believe as others, that it should be happening.

**"The World of Silence and the Silence You Shame"** this is the first Poem I had Published in any way. And since then it has been seen in a few places. It's also one of the Poems I read in my first public speaking since school. It's a powerful Poem for me, because it sums up my life so far. I felt the release after this one came out. You don't need to name names and put yourself at risk. I know who it's all about. And when they see it, so do they. I'm not saying don't name names but remember you have to be ready, the system can be one sided. It, many of us feel is not leaning towards us, but them.

**"C.M.H.T."** this is another example of getting your point across through writing. And unlike the enemies you fight, doing it in a constructive way which helps yourself and others. All contained within this piece is how it was for me and far too many. And only true accountability will ever change that.

**"Johns Gone"** this was at a time when the first person who helped me and seemed to understand had to leave, just a few months after we met. It left me needing to see someone else. And the new person wanted me to go through the Abuse with them from the start which was re opening the pain of doing it all over again. I wanted to just take up where I had left off. It is not that the person didn't care. But it did get to me and so that's why I wrote this.

**"The Survivor"** it says it all but because it's so positive it's worth remembering and mentioning again.

**"For You Louise"** This was written at a time I was struggling. And my mind, where it is such a minefield started giving me thoughts of a little spastic girl who died at seven years old. I was about fourteen I think. It was painful and what made it worse is, after writing this letter to her I wanted to visit her grave and place it there. But my head is so bad with blocks and trauma that sometimes I either remember everything or nothing. I tried but couldn't remember where she was buried even though I had gone to the funeral. Trying to remember in the end just hurt my head. So I couldn't go to her grave. But the letter is out there Louise. x

**"Surviving It, Us and Them"** this is so important and shows why, it is so important to survive. And something I feel very strongly about, like many things, how crucial it is we support each other. We are at our low points at different times. Just show our support for each other. Maybe a hello, an email or in whatever way you can. We together can take so much strength from that. And after receiving the opposite too much within the system, only ever makes it more important to know and do. And I don't know about you. But making a difference to another person is one of the only ways for me to feel self worth. It's a beautiful feeling. And it's yours to have. All you have to do is show it to someone else, whose worthy of it, just like YOU are.

**"Our Mother"** This is in here mainly because I don't think it's an accident with the link between my real Mum and Dad. The way it goes on about the true love of *a mother*. At a time I was battling with the horror of it all (Abuse). And the very painful betrayal, but love I do have for my mum, that I struggle with because of all the true facts that did emerge. That only ever made that love, painful, and harder for me to accept. And it was easier to *say* I hate my Dad, but I don't. It's almost like I was battling through it in this Poem, still being in denial. And that's why I find it interesting myself. Maybe I'm wrong.

70

**"For what you now witness..."** OK, now ones like this it is important for me to put them in. Yes. But equally it is important for me to go through a few facts of now. I am still alive and I wrote this maybe five years ago. So that's a positive thing to remember and know. Yes what this is about is obvious but there's more to it than that. At the time I wrote this, clearly I was at a low point. It was so bad that I was Fantasizing about my own death. I think a lot of it in a way was to hurt myself. Punish myself as much as anything. Sad times, I remember thinking about my death in my head and then near death (in my head) having a smile across my face, Sad. This piece came to me as I thought about other people in those situations left behind but this was out of thinking about the ambulance people who'd come in. And so I thought of this as to give some but little comfort to them, for as to what they would now see, a man in a bath of blood. IT WAS NEVER GOING TO HAPPEN. But these disturbing thoughts were there. And this is how it came out of me.

And also at this moment thinking to myself that as in life I would do everything to limit the damage to others. Thinking if I were to write on that wall, the blame, who and why. There would be no wall big enough. But I wouldn't want to hurt anyone anyway. But like I said it never came close. I am here. And this like the other things has a place here. And it is not negative. If it would have happened yes it would have been. I hope you see that through, yes the sadness, but is it not love of something or someone that would give the thoughts for others at this time. Even though it was in my head it still means something I believe. But you decide. After all that's what I want. Let's end this section on the title of...

**"My Saviour"** and let's just let that be true.

***The Writings on The Wall . . .*** All what you see in this section is the things that I wrote on the walls of my flat in my front room. Things were bad and I couldn't cope. This was the one and only time this happened. It has to come out in some way. I found myself writing stuff on the walls. Mostly about, CMHT, Family, Abuse, basically a lot of anger and pain. I was suffering on my own, and I was very isolated. After a few days I managed to get it together a bit, but before I got rid of it all (which took a lot of scrubbing) I decided to write it all down. So this is what I had written:-

<u>2005</u> NEW PEOPLE NEW THINGS
OUT WITH THE OLD. THEY SAY BETTER
THE DEVIL YOU KNOW. NA FUCK THAT
AT LEAST BE SOMETHING OLD DONE BY
SOMETHING OR SOMEONE NEW

\*\*\*

JUST WAITING FOR THE TIME
TO EXPOSE YOU DRs AND LIKE
NO MATTER WHAT. WHAT IT TAKES
OR DOES. KNOW AINT OVER WHILE I
BREATHE. **A** STOOD FOR SOMETHING **E** DID
**X** SHALL STAND FOR EXPOSURE DAY OF
US & DEM. WHAT I LIVE FOR. WITH OUT
WHICH I WOULD BE JUST LIKE YOU THEM

\*\*\*

I KNOW WHERE YOU'RE ALLEGIANCE LIES
ACTION SPEAKS LOUDER THAN WORDS
YOU WANT ME TO BELIEVE DIFFERENT
WHEN YOU BELIEVE IN THEM NOT ME
US. YOURSELVES AND THEM

\*\*\*

A NEW DAY **IS** DAWNING
AND WE WILL ALL FIND OUT IF
THAT'S A GOOD THING OR NOT WONT <u>WE?</u>

72

# Mad

Mad am I?
No it's Mad
You're Mad
I'm not mad
Because I know the difference
That's why they may think I am
But I know who
I was.
<u>What I am</u>
And the same about them
That's why they'd like me to be Mad
Or at least
People think it
It works
For them

\*\*\*

FATHERLESS
MOTHERLESS
BELIEVED TO BE
WORTHLESS

\*\*\*

IM AN ORPHAN
I HAVE NO FAMILY
ONLY LIARS AROUND ME
Drs OF DEATH AND SUFFERING PAIN
& TORTURE. SCUM.YOU'D LIKE THEM
YOU'D BELIEVE THEM LIKE YOU DO HAVE DONE
& CONTINUE TOO

YOU ADD TO THE
PAIN IN MY HEAD
YOU PERVERTED SCUM
YOU LOVE SUFFERING AND
TORTURE.YOUR SICK

\*\*\*

IM A FAT BASTARD AGAIN
MORE FRONT THAN MOST
WOMEN

\*\*\*

BELIEVE IN THEM
NO MATTER WHAT IT DOES TO US. CAUSE YOUR
ALWAYS RIGHT AREN'T YOU
ALWAYS INNOCENT OF ANYTHING
UNLIKE US A

\*\*\*

There were a couple of things I took out but most of it is here. It's important to show, I believe. I want people to see the rough and the smooth, the confident and the Doubting. We are real and these are normal emotions, thoughts and feelings, some of you / us, are going through.

To me, more than anything this shows that when you, me, them or anyone suppresses it. It builds up and something has got to give... or it forces its way out sooner or later ready or not. In this instance it came out in writing and the choice was not mine. Sometimes before and since it came out in anger towards stereos or guitars, which eventually didn't survive... but I did and so even though some may think it's destructive, it needed to come out. I was alone, I was scared, I, at times thought I was going to die but worse was how. I was going out of my mind I couldn't cope. I had no one. It's weird when I look back at what I wrote. But to me it shows how powerful Poetry is. Do you notice amongst all that anger and scribbling the Poem **"Mad"**?

# The Axis of Abuse

Their world
Which you exist in
All paths lead to them
All start with them

Where there's...
Nowhere to run too
Nowhere to hide
No one to turn too
No one's gonna come
No one ever does
Except him

Your world doesn't revolve around the sun
It revolves around their abuse
Of their activities of the day
And the nightmare's of your night

*This was inside a Picture I created, one of those A4 Posters you do. And my spelling showed through, as in wrongly. But the point or message which is the most important came across.*

# The Difference a Day Makes

Today was like yesterday
Yesterday was like… the day before
Being as it was about the past
So today was like other days
It visits me, when I don't visit it…
The past
Tomorrows another day
Maybe it will be different
Unlike today and other days
I hope so… that'll be a day
One I want to see
One I want to be
A day to remember
If it comes or when it comes
I know what I'll call it
I'll call it today
And hope tomorrow will be like today
So it won't mess up today
When I remember it
And it won't visit me
And I won't visit it
Like those other days
That today and yesterday
Will start to make up for it
And I can enjoy today
And I won't mind waiting
For tomorrow to come
Because today's a day
That I just don't want to end
Because today's the day
That I want to remember and savour
And that's the difference
A day makes

# But Still I Love Them

I don't hate my mum; I love her I can't tell her what she has done. Sometimes I come close to tell her I know, or lash out with that I know. But I can't. I love her so much like a mum that I always believed she was, and not the person she was and is. I love her, that's why it hurts so much. Like a dad I never had, brothers, family still no matter what. I love them and it hurts more and more, my head, the pain, my ill health, mentally, physically, in all ways. The pressure inside my head and heart, bursting feels like it will explode. My disorder that just plays it all out to much over so many things. The people I care or love the innocent that it affects that I do not see now. That I feel even they blame me because they don't know the real truth and so on the outside it looks so different to them. And you can't tell them because you don't want to hurt those innocent ones, but the guilty as well. Meanwhile some of the guilty tell their lies, the innocent not knowing believe, it all just adds to it. Every moment of everyday it kills you in every way it nearly has physically, the strain, trauma. Yet still you know like I do now, all said and done, I love them. That's why it hurts so much. And why it makes it all worse for me.

# The Lines Been Drawn

The lines have been drawn some are being drawn. I tried my best to avoid all out confrontation. It defeats us all. There are no winners, only losers, singularly or collectively as people, organisations and as a society. But if it cannot be avoided, then we must face it. And fight it for an end result that we all may at least learn from. So we can, stop it, prevent it, or to at least acknowledge it, if it happens again. We don't fight to win. We live in the knowledge in some ways we will lose. But we will lose much more if we don't fight it. So we fight to at least expose the facts and reveal the truth of the situation of both sides. And hope when it's all over we can begin to rebuild bridges between us. And make it work for who it should, and how it should.

# Hang in There

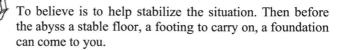

To believe is to help stabilize the situation. Then before the abyss a stable floor, a footing to carry on, a foundation can come to you.

So hang in there and believe, if only at first in you, it's a start. Doubt not yourself or your ability. It can come and will come believe it. For it to happen it's a must. Doubting it is nearing the abyss. Believing it is bringing the solid foundation that we need to carry on. So we don't just hang in there. That day comes when we are there.

## Out There Eyes

See too much
Too much going on
In here and out there
They've seen too much
Known too much
It becomes too much
You can see it
In their eyes
You can see it, feel it
In your eyes
Out there eyes
More about what's in
Than out
From them out there
All around
That gives you
That look
That stare
Of those…
Out there eyes

# The Rut

Why is it always tomorrow?
And not today
When you're in a rut
You just can't seem to get out of

You have to look at yourself
And be honest
Your gonna be in that rut
Until you do today

Don't wait for tomorrow
Tomorrow never comes
So realize that
And do it today

And then do it everyday
Face it. Do it
Don't just think it
Know it and believe it

Not I might or maybe
I WILL TODAY

And you'll find yourself
Out of that rut
Today not tomorrow
That's what you want, from today

# I / We

I'm going to kill that little boy, that way we won't suffer no more. The end will be slow but it will be an end, whether in peace or not. The Reality it will be in death like our lives... pain. I / We came into this world alone, I / We lived it alone and I / we will die alone. In starvation it will be like our life, long, drawn out and painful, amongst other things. That could fill more than this page, more than a book, more real than a film. For this is life, death. That cannot be portrayed. Because this is real and a portrayal of it is too lose sight of the fact and reality the feeling and more. A portrayal of it takes away the hard hitting reality and the facts. And makes it seem almost serial, portrayal is betrayal. For this is REAL and the reality of how it really feels. For I / We.

# The Waiting Game

Years go by. You must be patient playing the waiting game, on and on going nowhere, sideways, backwards, forwards to where you were. Nowhere, round and round in circles going, moving but getting nowhere. Minutes, hours, days, months, years go by, infuriating, bitter, anger and all, and so many things. Playing the waiting game, but only because you have no choice, but to play the waiting game, their waiting game. Ain't no fucking game their waiting game, you lose they win. You go out of your mind or feel it on your way to losing it. Then they win. Waiting, it's not just people going by and getting on with their lives while you cannot. For those that it's not their fault you wish it was different. Bitter not at them or you are but you try not to be. Waiting, waiting, and those who have and make it this way, they get on with their lives. While they make you, us play the waiting game. Fucking you up as more than people pass you by, but life itself and you, your intelligent enough to know time passed, you can't get back. I just want to have a chance to get a life and try to live, and that even if it happened, that would be hard enough. But they won't let you. You can't carry on because you need something, and until then, you can't go forward so as always you have to wait you have no choice. This is hell this waiting. And it ain't no game it's your life and it's passing you by. Or even worse one day it has passed you by and you have no time left. Their game is over like your life. Because that's what it always was. Not the waiting game, but your life.

81

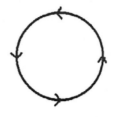

## The Vicious Circle

Don't be the beginning of it
Be the end of it
At the very least
Don't maintain it
Don't escalate it
Don't accelerate it
Face it
Too end that circle
Cope with it to break its cycle
So you can recycle your energies
To make your own circle
A positive one
To break out, get out
Of that…
Old used to be
But no more
Vicious circle
Because the circle has changed
YOU have changed it
And a new one has begun
One that leads to fun

## The Children of the Damned

We are... are we?
Because of you
Not because of we
The children of the damned
Damned by you
Damned if we do
Damned if we don't
That is what you have made our lives
In this...
Damnation
Damn you
But if we are indeed
The children of the damned
Then we must at least
Take solace in the fact
That we are THE CHILDREN
And you are...
The Damned


## Search Not Settle or the Searchers End

It may not feel or seem like it. But it's better to live life looking for what you want even though or when it seems it will or may never happen, than settling for what you don't want. When that happens, you will never know or have the chance of what you want, whether that is a relationship or other things in life. The search may seem never ending but while you search for it at least there's a chance and hope. If you settle for what you don't want you end the search, the hope and the chance. And so end the happiness that would come if you keep searching and find and get what you want. So search with hope. Not settle for less and end the search. Let the search be at an end only when you find and get what you want. The searches end. Not an end to searching.

# An introduction to my next Poem

I found out I had been sexually Abused in childhood Five years ago (2003). I had been known to the CMHT before; I found out since then that they knew of my Family background. But because of a mental block of my childhood I didn't know nothing was clear. In January of that year, while trying to sort out another part of my traumatic head. I sadly had it confirmed that something that was buried in my head did happen. I then began to know it was a flashback which I had had in earlier years but it made no sense to me then. But I had become aware of it again in recent years and so spoke of it to someone who confirmed it as a fact, though it made no sense to me until it was definitely confirmed. Though previous relationships with CMHT had broken down, I at that moment thought this would be different. How wrong could I be? I even had a little faith in them left still despite everything that had gone on before. It does get to you when they do so go on about trust. Yet they show themselves that they are not to be trusted. Which leads them to say can't help you; you need to trust and so on and so on. Even I did not think they would turn me away yet again. Offer drugs and go away you know the one. A friend at the time took me down to see them because of the problems I

 have with them. And there was this person who has headed up my local CMHT for years since (which I struggle with) there with someone else. I was supposed to be assessed by a Psychiatrist. She had no intention of helping me. For thirty odd years I had never been angry even when I should have been. My friend said "I've never seen John like this". Leading up to this because of my deterioration of health and the frustration among other things (including events and circumstances) I had begun to be angry, which is good though I

don't like it. It is healthy like all things when in an appropriate way. In the end I had to get out. After I left she said to my friend "all I can see is anger" Please I'm not going to go there from the little you read you as a decent person make a deduction. I'm sure it will be different... o.k. I'll go there a bit. Well I just found out my whole life had been a lie. I couldn't comprehend it all my mind couldn't take it. I was surrounded by people who knew when I didn't, not just family. Yet again I was being turned away. That day a GP when I begged for help said "he is a danger to himself and more likely others" I was a mess. I was so scared frightened. I couldn't trust myself having urges to slit my wrists. People say "oh he won't" makes no difference to the trauma you feel. When you fear someone may hurt you. You may be able to get away you may not. If that person is in the same room, that's a problem. If you maybe that person. That is scary. You in any situations like it learn what true fear is, if you didn't before. Especially if there is a part of you who like me then doesn't want to die. So this is dedicated to you head of CMHT and all others like her where ever you are. I can't apologize for the sarcasm, because you so richly deserve it.

## Questionable Anger

Anger... No?... Why?
Must I be happy I was Abused?
Have I no reason to feel Angry?
I don't understand
If so
Why is it OK for you to be Angry with me?
But I mustn't be at them?
Or now you?
Isn't Anger a normal response?
Why must you make me feel...
Like I am not normal?
Just because I feel this way
As you know
It does make me Angry
Isn't that what you wanted to avoid?
I'm not an angry person
I'm a Person... who is Angry
I believe there is a difference
Don't you?
No... not you
Because we're both Angry now
I'm asking
YOU

85

# Accountable

You say we are
You say you are
Accountable, Accountable
Oh to *all* be...
Accountable

There are ways
To make us if we're not
Accountable, Accountable
Oh to all be *made*...
Accountable

I don't see you
But you've seen me
Accountable, Accountable
No one makes *you*...
Accountable

I'm sorry
Is this the right verse?
Accountable, Accountable
Oh the day when you *are*...
Accountable

# Someone Once

He was someone once
It wasn't me
It was make believe
Now I see
What I don't want to see
It has not changed me
It has made me
That's why there was
A make believe
All the good inside
Is just so painful
This is someone
I don't want to be
These are things
I don't want to have
Happened to me
Oh know
Here we go
Back to make believe
I was someone once

## To The Grave

It's not so much that you want to take it to your grave. It's that you are willing for it to take us to our graves. It shows the type of person you are. That only adds to what you did, are doing and will continue to do, forgiveness? What you did, the type of things would be enough in itself. That you blame us denies it to yourself. Selfish are you in the true meaning absolutely are you. So forgive me? For not what I feel or think of you. But what I know about YOU.

## Waiting for Something to Happen

Feels like it will never happen, but it does, so often, too often, but not what you want. Not what you need. But the reason, the cause of why you were waiting for something to happen, but something else, not this. "All comes to he who waits"? So they say. Well I have, we have and we still wait. IT happens. What we want, what we need doesn't happen. Maybe it will never happen, never this way any way. Maybe it's then you painfully realize. Waiting is all we may ever do. We better make sure. Time to… MAKE IT HAPPEN.

\*\*\*

DAYTIME IS THE TIME FOR LIVING
NIGHT TIME IS THE TIME OF DREAMING

**"Mad"** from *The Writings on the Wall Section*. This section actually has its own write up but this Poem needs to be mentioned. I was within the situation of, at one time my enemies within the CMHT saying I'm fine. And my other enemies "nudge nudge wink, wink, you know he's..." you can fill in the blanks. When someone is referred to in these ways like people saying they are Mad, a Nutter or not all there. It's a way of them discounting anything that person ever has to say, in one final blow. And what's worse is, once you have this label, No one needs to reissue it, as well as that specifically if they (anyone) label you with Depression of any kind. Sadly people can again dismiss anything you've got to say very easily even if you've got a valid point. Sometimes no one will listen to you, which is so frustrating and adds to it all. And if you show your anger, displeasure then that can be used against you. (I've had this). For instance, this good councillor (I had) said something about part of the system that was bad. And it was. But I turned to him and said "but you can say that, I can't" he looked puzzled for a moment as I went on "because they will just say oh he's a Psychotic Depressive" and he understood that. But then that's what made him a good one. He listened. And judged what I had to say on its merit and merit alone. That's all I ask.

**"But Still I Love them"** that title says it all. But I just want to pick out this again to show throughout this book. People can and maybe deny it, but it's Love. And I want people to see this. I don't want the overriding impression to be pain and suffering. And if we are ever to gain more widespread active support within society we have to have this part expressed to.

**"Hang in There"** it's quite simple. But that's what I like. I believe this little thing and the funny little picture (that I did that wasn't meant to be funny I might add) is important. Sometimes whenever and where ever if you can, just talk in plain simple English, its best. I remember doing this I was talking about what I had done before, that gave me a chance. And it's again worth a mention because it is dealing with these issues, and there consequences, in a positive way. And expressing, HOPE. You can do it.

**"Out there Eyes"** This described how at some point I felt when I was taking tablets and self conscious of the certain look someone sometimes has when they are not quite with it. What for me made it even more significant is when I was being given highly addictive drugs that were not meant for long periods. I was really ill because of them. And for the one and ONLY time I called the Drs Out, in the out of hours surgery because I was so worried.

89

They came in, a man and he had a woman with him. This Poem was on the Coffee table with the picture of those eyes staring up from it, which for a brief moment I was paranoid about, but in the end was funny.

**"I / We"** this was written around the time when I had this thing about starving myself. It was *one* of the things that started to give me real problems about eating, food and about my weight. I need to add, killing the boy if you haven't realized is the boy I was. I was as you can tell very low, struggling, fantasizing about death then being scared of it. Laying there believing that I wanted to die. It was then that I thought to myself. "Well if you really do want to die. Then why do you eat?" so I began to punish myself about that. So I decided I was going to starve myself to death. No one noticed. That only made me feel worse. This went on for months two, three? In this time I barely ate and even if I had a biscuit or something I would hate myself for it. Continuing to tell myself "Why are you eating if you say you want to die?" over and over. It gave me serious long term issues about food, eating, when, where, how much, which I have problems with to this day. But there were two more reasons why eating and weight became a problem. But again as with the rest, this was written quite a few years ago. And I am still here.

**"The Waiting Game"** is definitely worth a mention. This is sad but completely accurate. And there are a few things I have written about waiting, wasting your life, existence. This particular one picks up on the Abusers of you, creating a forced silence outside and in. You can't get on because you need something. Something if you got from them i.e. their confession of guilt and, that they DID something to you, and acknowledgment that you were unjustly treated. It would help and show that there are reasons why you have the problems you do. You are suffering through no fault of your own. And in my case it was some of the Health Service Personnel, of the ones and type I had the sad misfortune of coming across, which had made it worse. They don't represent what the NHS is all about. But without proper accountability they will and have corrupted it, its values and its purpose. I never did anything to warrant the lack of care or even compassion that their attitudes inflicted on me. Maybe one day these people will be shown their place... on that day they won't be anywhere near the Health Service or anybody whose purpose is to CARE. And that's what is so sad in my and some others story's. It's what we have endured on top of our Child Abuse through the System and Health Service, that I do believe in. That's why it hurts and disturbs me so much.

**"The Children of the Damned"** The fact is when you think about it. There may be only one letter difference between us, the Abuse*d* and the Abuse*r*. But as we know, it makes all the difference. So if we are low and we relate to The Children of The Damned, don't dwell on The Damned. Know who you are. *You were WRONGED. They ARE wrong*. And that's what makes this Poem true. Just like **"Our Silence"** in the previous section.

**"Accountable"** that's what I want to see of them. It says it all in this Poem. That I sat down and wanted to write. Good or not doesn't matter to me. It is something that I want, accountability. We are, time for them to be. A lot of people will tell you that they are. "They" mainly in this case actually being bad Drs and People within the Health Service who are not *made* accountable enough. You find one of the only times within the Health service they are, is when it's a good one being mistreated because they blew the whistle on someone or something that was going on. I BELIEVE in OUR health service and so with others will continue to expose it. And demand change.

**"Someone Once"** another Poem of being lost, but fighting being found, because it's not how you want it to be. And that makes it such a hard journey whether you've got a Mental Block or not. Some may not understand but think of it this way. Would you be in a rush to know all that happened to you if you were sexually abused? It's not something that you're ever going to want to have happened to you. And it's a natural instinct to resist it. That's what makes denial so powerful. And the expressions like "you only hear what you want to hear" and "you only see what you want to see". Which can and is true of most of us at times, and especially within this context.

**"To the Grave"** the truth of this hurts so much especially when it's done by people you love. I will say no more about this piece. It would detract from it.

Well by the end of these pieces I had started to become in contact with NAPAC. Somewhere near the end of 2008. So who is NAPAC? They are a National Charity. It's The National Association for People Abused in Childhood. And it is significant to me because I came across them on the internet. I took a chance having no experience of them. Glad I did. After looking at their website I saw that you could send your Poems in. And so I sent in **"The World of Silence and the Silence You Shame"**. Having sent it in (via email) at first I was worried when I didn't hear back. But I needn't have. Up it went on their website. Tears came to my eyes. I was so moved

91

and there was a little pain to, because of what it was all about. But it was a beautiful moment I will never forget it and I was and am so glad I did it. For the first time I had my say. It was out there. Ok yes I have said things before but this was different. I hope if anyone who is in a safe enough place to do this and does. That it can give you the same feeling. And if you don't or cant, that's ok. If I speak and you agree then know and believe you speak through me or anyone else who speaks out. This is about US through you and me. Together we sadly share in the pain when things are bad. But please share in the good when we get somewhere to. Over the next few months I submitted some more Poems, Prose and Pictures to. I read others work on there and still do. I am now going to leave it at that for now. Because at the end of the book I want to go into some more positive details about NAPAC and other things I have and are doing right now.

From now on what you will see was all written from 2009. I have a particular reason to separate this section at this Point from the rest which I can discuss at the end of it. But what I can say now is, it's especially because for me and my writing it was a very significant, positive year. I wrote just less than thirty Poems and only two Prose. As Poetry *is* my outlet now.

# What's the Point?

I lay here in bed after all these years in pain... with tears... traumatized. Some of the pain is needless. Thirty eight years of Abuse. It's not stopped yet. "What's the point?" You have to ask. When you are at an end or seem to be. But the question isn't asked, it like the flashbacks or memories through them, Visits YOU. "What's the point?" You battle with it. Often you can't seem to tell the truth and answer it. It's like sometimes you lie to get by. Maybe if things improve you can ask "What's the point?" and you can have an answer. And on you go forward. But I've been there too. "What's the point?" Tears welling up in my eyes I fear I know the answer. So much pain, so alone, so much victimized so much wrong. "What's the point?" An answer is in me. I know it's not good. It's like a silent answer, one that wells up more tears. But the denial of the answer right now keeps me safe. Can so many for so long be all wrong? Hey another question, reasoning the unreasonable. Can I be so wrong to believe they Abuse me and it is wrong? Why do so many not act when they know? They are so absent. They believe those that hurt us, the lies, the miss truths, the half truths. "What's the point?" I keep fighting it and them. But where does it get me? Back here again. "What's the point?" But here's another question I ask and I know the answer too. What else is there? If I don't. OH it could be worse. It's all hard to live with exist with. But if I don't fight it and them, how could I live with it? I couldn't. "What's the point?" NO. Fight it with "What else is there?" That's the point. I hope it keeps you safe too.

## The Ranting Post

It's a rant
A post that's down
Well this post might seem a bit down
But it's the truth
Recent cases of child abuse
The result for the abuser
The end result for the abused
The never ending result for us
Same old, same old
Like me, like us, like them

You could write a poem about it
We have
You could write a book about it
We have
You could make a film about it
We have
They could do something about it...
We wait

Harsh?
Harsh is the affliction of it
Harsh is the injustice of it
Harsh is that no one deserves it
Yet it happens everyday
Harsh is to always endure
Harsh is to be told we are Harsh
Because we see no end
And we tell it so
Have we all the answers? No
But who listens to the ones we have?
Have they all the answers? No
Did we ever think they did?
How long have they been at it?
How long till there's a change?
Sorry for the chain of questions

It's because of the chain of events,
The lack of a difference
And who suffers when they fail?
They should know…
It's what makes us who we are
To tell the tale
If only they would listen

"Flashback"

Names have been changed apart from my own, to Protect the?

***Situation... Distress.*** John's in his flat that he moved into recently that year. His friend Jane is there. John is struggling with the recent realization of being a victim of Child Abuse, and of not being helped by the ones that should. He feels bursts of anger within through frustration and shear helplessness. He's talking to Jane. She is his sounding board. But not enough tonight as he grabs a table from his bay window and throws it across the room. It break's as it hits the floor. Jane is scared for John. John is scared. Why won't they help him? What next? Jane is concerned as she has been before so she rings casualty. The nurse talks to Jane. John hears but doesn't hear. Then Jane asks John questions. John doesn't know what the Fuck to say. He's Fucked and needs help is all he really knows right now. It's too much. Jane hands John the phone. The nurse speaks. John isn't up to this. He looks at Jane and hands her the phone. "I don't know what she's on about" he says. Jane talks. Apparently the Doctor won't come and see John... too dangerous. So Jane takes John up to casualty. Jane and her husband Dave are good friends. The only ones Johns got right now. Its evening as they arrive at casualty. John is walking with his hands on his head pushing against his temples the pain in his head it's just too much. Shortly after arriving they enter a small room off the waiting area. Dr Why is sitting down, stuff is said. John feels like the Doctor is saying that John is blaming everyone else for his misfortune. John is angry at this. It's not like that. He paces the short distance of the room. He goes too near the door for Jane's liking. He might leave. She stands in his way in case he does. He turns and continues pacing again. He's very distressed. He says what he always says when these situations take place, the truth how it is, how he feels. But these situations are far too familiar to him. Just like the end result has become and whose fault it is. Dr Why says "They won't see him when he's like this" Unbelievable. More stuff is said. Now they wait for what's next. John exits the room while they wait for the answer. Holding his head again hands pressing on his temples elbows high he walks around the corner, slumping down on the floor in a long corridor. Still with hands against his head pushing his temples crying, as he turns to the right slightly angles his head up to see Jane looking on. Standing at the beginning of the corridor she's as helpless as he is to do anything. He knows that look. He himself has had that look as he looked on at someone in distress and people wouldn't help them too. Shortly afterwards she takes him in the car to hospital (again). Talking to John she is trying to get **him** to behave so they will now finally help him. But within days the outcome that was already

96

decided, has been decided. As they tell him that he isn't ill and doesn't need their help. And now must go home.

Remember only the names have been changed. Now what was it Dr Why said? "They won't see him when he's like this". Let's break that statement down. It's not a word game. But let's fill in the details.

They - The Mental Health

won't see him - won't see John

when he's like this. - when he's in Mental Distress.

So now what was it that Dr Why was actually saying?

**"The Mental Health won't see John, when he's in Mental Distress."**

***

<u>Poetry & the Survivor Survive</u>

POETRY NEEDS TO SURVIVE

Survivor's poetry... shows us that it can

Just like us

# The Prisoner Outside and In

Can you see these bars?
Confine us deep within

They're all around
Outside and in

They are the strongest bars
That a man ever made

They are not heavy these bars
But the burden carrying them

As I think to myself
How long has it bin?

Since the day I seemed to...
Take it on the chin

It's been too long
With too long to go

You can't see these bars
But in these words I bet you hear

For I am the prisoner
Outside and in

For too long I know
Has it bin

# The Fantasist

They said I was a fantasist
Something they'd missed
I did try to resist
But it did persist

I tried so hard
With everything I had
I tried so hard
With everything I hadn't

They said I was a fantasist
They did insist
It was put on a list
It does exist

I wished they'd help
I wished it was different
I wanted to believe
But in the end, it did deceive

They said I was a fantasist
What they do led to this
I wished and I wished
For this and this

What they're about
It seemed so unreal
So off I went, in search
For something I could feel

They'd created a fantasist
Its all I had just to exist
For their help I tried to enlist
That's what makes me, a fantasist

# An Impression of Depression

Isolated
Very alone
The only place I roam
Is in my home
Down
Very down
To get to the bottom of this?…
I don't know
But I am at bottom
Rock bottom
When you know the only way is up
When you feel like giving up
Pain so severe
You can feel this pain year on year
Your hurt has led to this
Now you're surrounded by an abyss


Sick
Sick right through
Sick of everything inside of you
Sick of everything you do
You don't amount to much
People think… why you make so much fuss
Right now these thoughts fill you
In everything you do
Sometimes it overflows
This is the time you must show
What you have got, to survive
That's why you're still alive
It has showed itself to me
As I start again to believe

I feel it grip
As I tighten it
I'm pulling myself off the floor
To try and do some more
I'm rising *up* high
Not too much to touch the sky
Gotta keep it reigned in
So it's not just a spin
This is very real
And not just how I feel
So here I am once more
I just hope
There's no encore


## The Honesty of Love & the Ending of it


"How was it for you?"
"You're the best I've had so far today"
A lust of love that never ends

"How was it for you?"
"I've had better"
The end of a romance
And a murmur of a love
That could have been

"How was it for you?"
A question thought
But never asked
A love that is deceived
As required
An acknowledgement of togetherness
No matter what

And someone who knows better

## To Who and Why

I am writing to the Prime Minister
I'm trying to air the silent voice
But there is no one there

I am writing to the Prime Minister
I'm trying to break the silence
But there is no one to hear

I am writing to the Prime Minister
Just to let him know
That I am still here

I am writing to the Prime Minister
I let him know that we won't be ignored
And we will never get board

I am writing to the Prime Minister
Telling him of the current situation
But through, shear frustration…

I am writing to the Prime Minister
Hoping one day that he will hear
He hasn't… he won't is my fear

So today…

I am writing to the Prime Minister
While he is still that
Because unlike him
What I am I will always be

Until we set each other free

# Someone's Gonna Come

You lay there hoping
Someone's gonna come
And make it all better
Someone's gonna come
And things will be different
But no one comes
It hurts
It gets you down
You have to believe
That something will change
You believe in yourself
They don't believe in you
But someone's gonna come
How else will it change?
I do all I can
But it's not enough
Someone's gonna come
Surely?
Because…
I need someone to come
To help
And together
We can make it different
And we can make a difference
Someone's gonna come
They have to
While I can still believe

# They

They lay in wait for me
With answers to questions never asked
With rebuffs to lies never questioned

They lay in wait for me
In a life I've always known
One that I've never sewn

They in wait, I'm in a state
Quick, quick as I make a break
I outwit them
As I outwit myself

They lay in wait for me
In an endless world of sorrow
It seems it will be tomorrow
Like a diver rising for air
But knowing they will be there

They lay in wait for me
As I stand here alone
Sometimes I feel myself grown
Feeling the pain
And knowing of its strain

You may not be aware
You may not think
They're even there
But they are
They are never far

They lay in wait for us
Us, Us
As for a moment, one alone
Becomes many alone
For those moments of being aware
Of each other's despair

They lay in wait...
For YOU


## Behind Closed Doors


The Door closed shut
Democracy, was hidden from view
Now that the door is shut
We can have secret Justice
No one will see
The Pain and Loss
Not least of all...
Democracy
It's been done in your name
Is this National Security?
The reason for these, closed doors?
Or is it
Insecurity
Theirs, not yours
What is it?
That they are doing
That needs to be
So secret from us
The door was opened
And we stood
Without a clue
This?... Democracy
So hidden from YOU

*About the Secret Family Court's, "Where is the openness of Democracy?"*

# Consumed Within

Stop it, stop it
Consumed within
Stuck in a loop, stuck in a loop
Loopy loo, loopy you
I got things to do

I'm doing them, I'm doing them
As I try to get on, I'm stuck in this thread
I write this here in my bed
There's something that just has to be said
I can see myself do it. I can see myself do it
Over and over, I feel it's taking over
I'm out. I'm out, nothing to shout about
I'm in; I'm in, as it starts to begin
Again and again, Oh not again
I feel like I'm going insane
I do a Poem, I read a poem
I read it again...
And again, and again

Stop it, stop it
Consumed within
Stuck in a loop, stuck in a loop
Loopy loo, loopy you
I got things to do

I'm planning my way out
Conspiring against myself
By myself, by myself
I've got myself convinced
This is it, this is it
I know what I must do
I'm on my way out
This isn't like before
This is different
I will start life again

106

But I only get to think it
Over and over, Again and again
Like a momentous train
Floundering where it started
Never ending, just starting
Would you pay for a fair?
Starting from where you started
On a continuous track
A never ending one at that
This is no journey to be on

Stop it, stop it
Consumed within
Stuck in a loop, stuck in a loop
Loopy loo, loopy you
I got things to do

Where am I now?
Out of the loop, or on route
We will see
It wouldn't be so bad
But the truth is sad
When I wasn't in this loop
Life still wasn't good
Being on my own, Talking to myself
Only myself, a lonely loner
Who at times felt like life was over
He began to plan
Oh such a glorious plan
To get back on track
To where he thought, it might be at
He thought. He tried
Not getting there he tried
Again and again
It's a loop of its own
One I don't want to be home

Stop it, stop it
Consumed within
Stuck in a loop, stuck in a loop
Loopy loo, loopy you
I got things...
*I do want* to do


## The Psychiatric Window


Standing at the window
Wearily watching, gazing on
As it all went passed
I stand still, paused

Yesterday the highlight of my day
Was staring at the coke machine
Sitting on a sofa
Most of the day, long, long

Others shuffled past
Some like me, some not
You feel quite distant
Sometimes not

But today
I'm looking out the window
So wanting to be... out there
So today I guess I'm lucky
That when I look out the window
I see something else
Other than, my own stare

# Dead Poets

They killed them.
They revived the ones they loved
And made dead ones of
Ones they didn't even know
They mocked the mocking birds
Oh I know it sounds absurd
I thought I was ok
You see
I'm a writer first
But they soon righted that
Lucky I'm not a poet
Poetically I'd be dead
I got this stuff in my head
Sometimes it comes out
I write a story or two
Gibberish, allsorts to bemuse
Sometimes poetry
*ssshhh*
It seems it must be free
Of inside of me
It has something to say
It touches, you feel
And it can heal
Some try and conceal
But even a dead poet can't do that
Poetic Justice me thinks
Agh you see
That's why
Poetry isn't dead

# The Emptiness of Hunger

There's a sensation in your stomach
From denying yourself food
You feel an achievement
Well done, you know?
As a wry smile appears on your face


Self neglect, self harm?
What does it matter?
If you cared it wouldn't be anyway
Do you know of that gladness?
From within of hurting yourself
It's a side effect that only ever helps


You're close to weightlessness
You're well on your way to size nothing
For you it's the only one that will do
You're convinced
For size zeros far too big for you

Some slash, some dash
Some throw up, for some... times up

But is it a numbness in your stomach?
Or a numbness to your pain
An indifference to you, from you
After an emptiness they left you


But your gonna teach everyone a lesson
You'll hurt yourself so much
It will numb out the pain
Their pain, your pain, all pain
That'll set it right

It's been so long
That hurting yourself
Is something you've become used to
A form of escape, controlled by you
Oh yeah...
You've convinced yourself of that too


## Wasting


I'm waiting for something
Something and it will click
Today came but it didn't happen
Just like yesterday
Then today's as good as over
Now I'm just passing through
Sitting and waiting
Waiting for the time to pass
Waiting
Wanting for tomorrow
So it can happen, and I can get on
Doing nothing else
Wasting these moments
No. Wasting the day
One day to two
Two to three
Not minutes to
But wasted days
Stuck in loops
Stuck in a rut
Wasting time
Its wasting
You're wasting
Wasting your life
Wasting away

# The Rock

I crawled from under a rock
To be here today
It seems so harsh to say
From so very far away
From my comfort zone
My rock, my home
I was only doing what you wanted
You wanted me to be seen
And not heard
You know it well enough
So it's not so absurd
But to you it seemed
so easy
You could block me out
Easy peasy
But every now and then
The others heard of us
One or two even
Created a fuss
Hush, hush I say
I was afraid
I didn't know what to do
What and where
It would lead too
You know I fear you
But you know I love you
For a moment I was so... visible
But then you came
And I disappeared
The silence was loud
So loud no one could hear
I hid alone with my fear
It was then that it came to me
As I crouched there
I saw the rock
So I crawled under it
Till you all forgot

I crawled from under a rock
To be here today
Oh I know, I know
What some of you will say
Why don't I crawl back?
Under my rock
The one that in time
Some forgot
But now I know
And I must tell you this
Face to face
I'm afraid I can't
For someone else
Has taken my place

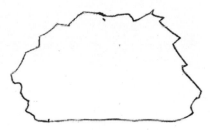

*This Poem is dedicated to NAPAC and all who are Raising Awareness of Child Abuse and its Consequences in Later Life.*

# Within The Silence

Clunk
And the shackles went on
I didn't even know it
What had I done wrong?

Drip, Drip
As my life fled away
It was all too late
Was it me who'd gone astray?

Crackle n Crack
As your life starts to shatter
Deserve it or not
It doesn't matter

Click
An unfastening belt
But this is for real
As you yelp

Smack, Whack, Crack
And not just words
We have the scars
But it goes unheard

A Silent Whimper
Of a love never lost
But these are people
You should never cross

A Smile
Oh happy I am
What a lie
Just like "I'm from Si am"

A Telling...
Of their love
Like a bedtime story
Is it all made up?

Hear, Listen
And be aware
There's a lot goes on...
Within this silence

*(The Reprise)*

Can you hear the scraping?
Can you hear the banging?
Can you hear the crying?
Can you hear the whimpering from the one next door?

Have you told yourself?
"They must be really bad kids.
Oh that's what it is"
But think...
Does anyone deserve to be treated like this?

When enough say no

We'll break this Silence

## She said / He said

She mocked me
With full intent
Her tongue like a razor
To slice right through me
Attack! Attack!

"This is not Poetry" she said
"It doesn't even rhyme"
As I turned to her and said

"By your command...
But my inner self
Is not on demand
It's not as fine
As the grains of sand
But also... not so bland"

She turned
Just like her look
She went away
And that was all it took

# The Other Side of Silence

There's another victim
And it's time to break the spell
Because you blame yourself
And I know that hell

So remember this...

It's not your fault
You did not hear
It's the silence created
Through the fear

It's not your fault
You didn't see
All the things
That they did to me

It's not your fault
You couldn't help
You were not there
When we yelped

It's not your fault
You didn't suspect
How were you to know?
With all due respect

It's not your fault
You didn't know
You believe you should have
So it's time for me to show

Through both sides of the silence
And to help you see
That you're a victim of it
Just like me

*Dedicated to the ones who would have... if they'd only have known*

# Blooming Vera

Oh Vera
Your soft clear voice
Tells of the white cliffs of Dover
That all shall see
When all this war is over


Oh Vera
Do you remember when
You told us
We will meet again
Don't know where
Don't know when
And though many
were laid down to rest
Best of this Island
From you
Oh God bless you
From us
You still hold true


Oh Vera
You sang to us
There will always be an England
Land a Free
The rolling hills
And plenty valleys deep
Oh yes this England
still is true
And Vera
This England still loves you

Oh Vera
Through the days
Of black and white reels
Through oh so many
Too many
Far away Poppy fields
Through sky's true and blue
And through dark shadows
Of yet more war
But we know our Vera's
Always ready
For the next encore


Oh Vera
This land
These cliffs
Those blue bells
The thatched roofed cottages
And red pillar boxes
Oh them all
Reminds us of this land
And we never forget
Where it all began
For our hearts were always filled
When you sang


*A Dedication to the Life and Works of Dame Vera Lynn*

# Air Time

This is my time
The time I've been waiting for
It's not time to settle a score
It's time...
We faced the facts
The reality itself
With us
Always interacts

That's why
We make a fuss
It's for real
The real deal

Believing or not
Doesn't stop it breaking us
Believing or not
Doesn't stop the pain
But not believing
IS PAIN...
Again and again
As before
More on more

Believing in us
Is a chance
One since so many
Never had
One so many
Never will
So many
Never can
We can never know why
It was just, never in the plan

But your belief in us
Is never too late
So today...
I'm gonna celebrate
You can celebrate too
Because we need each other
To make that true

Breaking the silence
Is the start
And hearing us
Is the only way
Because without it
We ain't got a say
And things would always be
The same old way

But today we spoke
And today you listened
This Air Time, Is our time
And make no mistake

IT'S TO BE HEARD


*This Poem came about just before I went on the Radio*


## Loves Not Lost On Me


I might be lost
Because of it
I might be lost
Without it
But it's not
Lost on me


121

# The Art of Being Lonely

Loneliness is Ugly...

Loneliness is a world full of people
Yet still being alone
Loneliness is a room full of people
Close
But never could be further away

Loneliness is finding it hard to say
"I am lonely"
Loneliness is not to be shared
Loneliness is the sharing of it...
But to still be lonely

Loneliness is in an over populated world
With lands empty of green spaces
Towns with houses packed side by side
With nowhere to hide
Where it won't find you
As loneliness consumes you

Loneliness is nosey neighbours
Offering to do favours
Just to find out more

Loneliness is in bright lit streets
With lots of noise
And a closing time
That brings the revellers out
While you are always in

Loneliness is cities with tower blocks towering
Reaching the sky
Like concrete fingers always pointing away
But still you are lonely
And still you are alone
Loneliness is miserable

Loneliness is people avoiding you
Like it's a disease they can catch from you
You have loneliness
You're a carrier
You are contagious always
You carry it with you
So they... stay away

Loneliness is to love God
And not feel loved
Loneliness is too much to bear

Loneliness is to be aware
That you're alone
But to have no answers for it

Loneliness is to be suddenly invited to places
Places you wouldn't go
With people
You don't even know
Loneliness is pitiful
Loneliness is Dark

Loneliness is to write a short Poem
That could have filled
So many pages more
Loneliness is for that Poem
To be called
The Art of Being Lonely
And for it to come from you
And be, Too true

Loneliness is not a forgotten Art
It's when...
Your worlds apart

# So Sad WAS I

I dialled a number
A soft voice spoke
And talked gently
I spoke tentatively at first
But then...
Not so hurried
This voice filled me with care
It comforted me
That I could be heard
Listening intently
Ever so gently
A voice of understanding
At last!...
A short time passed
As I gasped but...
The pain
The pain was no longer alone
This beautiful voice
Had filled me with warmth
And before I knew it
An hour was over
Time spent
Rebuilding my faith
I spared a thought
For the others
Of need too
For I could have talked all night
This voice would let me
This voice could hear me
This voice could see me
This voice told me all this
It was then I knew
That this voice said...
I was someone

*Thoughts of The Samaritans*

# If Not Now

Poppy fields now
Poppy fields then
Give it a year
Give it ten

The bombs still drop
The pain still follows
Makes what politicians say
Seem so hollow

Follow them there
Follow them then
I had something to say
So I took up my pen

Will a day ever come?
When it's not this way
With wars to end wars
That leads to yet more

I know we don't live
In an ideal world
But I can't help but want
To not lose, more boys and girls

Thought provoking
Not meant to cause offence
Poets you know
Can't sit on the fence

*Dedicated to all with Loss.*

# The Lost and Fallen

What has become of them?
Have they fallen in vain?
Some now head up campaigns
Reminding us all
Of their pain
Some in time
Sweep it aside
But never forgotten are they
By some of us
The telling of the wholeness
Of a sad story
But through it, the warmth that
They never died in vain
Others still feel the pain
Theirs along with their own
It's too close to home
What has become of the lost?
Many still too far away
Too far to have their say
We are the in-between
Amongst the rest of you
In full view
Sometimes we join together
We march
We write
We sing
We...
Do
So what of the lost and fallen?
We carry their light
Along with ours

# Geezer Non Poet

I'm a Geezer
Not a Poet
I'm a Geezer
Making time
To be sure to show it

A hidden Poet
Embarrassed to come out
His Poetry hidden
Forbidden or not
There's no doubt

The Peoples Poet
Poetry by the People
For the People
People, Poet... we are

Our Poems don't match up to theirs
Theirs don't match up to ours
Oh to be different
So what's so wrong with that?

Time to break these shackles
And speak of this... Poetry

"So, what type of Poetry do you write?"
"Poetry, perhaps you've heard of it?"
Merciless are they
So why not we?

We gotta take this Poetry back
A revolutionary fact
But don't worry
The only weapons you need
Are but, a Pen, Paper
And of course...
The Spoken word

# The Humble Phoenix

You're the Phoenix
Rising from the ashes
Rising high
Reborn, revived
The ashes from whence you came
They are not wasted
Returning to earth
Having given rebirth
Even the fire that had burned
Inside and out
And all around
Could not destroy you
It made you
Stronger, wiser
Turning you into something beautiful
Even if you don't see it
others do
Seems so strange
This Phoenix
So not spoken of
Since there must be so many
And many written of
Brought about
By so many... being written off
This Phoenix
Usually is humble
And will not except
Its own existence
Unless by another name
It's not seeking fame
It's been reborn
To live, live

And love again

## The Two Sides to the Poet

The Poet that don't even know it
We're so content to see
There just like you and me

And The Poet that does...
How much worse could it be?
Who we've, got no time to see

So watch out when your secrets out
Watch them scrambling for the doors

And as your Poem comes to an end
And you hope and reach
The time of applause

Spare a thought, for the ones

Who never made the doors




## Love

Love is holding someone close
And never wanting to let go
The best love...
Is never having too

# Love Is

Love is...
Loving them
Despite what they
Have done to you
Despite what they
Do to you
Despite what they
Will do to you

Love is...
Carrying on
Through the pain
Doing despite
Not having nothing to gain
Believing in them
Even when they
Don't believe in you

Love is...
A blindness to something
Or someone
That may get in its way
Giving someone a second chance
While others
Wouldn't have stood a chance

Love is...
Something that flows
Something that grows
Something to show
Burning inside
Like wild fire
But prettier
Than the prettiest flower

Love is...
So worthwhile
You only need to feel without it
Just for a while
To know how precious
It really is
Love is keeping the heart pumping
Making it more
Than just another pump

Love is...
Here
It's there
It's high
It's low
It can travel at the
Speed of light
In a moment
Making a moment
You want to last forever

Love is...
Something that's in you
Seeming to lay dormant
Visiting you
Most precious
When you're feeling blue
Powerful and tearful
Love is all this
And more

Love is, so wanting more

And again we're picking up on a few of the previous Poems with my take on them. Maybe they mean something different to you. If so, neither of us is wrong. Like a painting we can all see different things in the same Picture. All I hope is that it's a positive thing for you, about you or me, or just people becoming aware of all the issues involved in a constructive way. I want nothing less than that, to come from all of this.

Well as I said before all the previous writing in this last section was done from 2009, lets mention the first piece **"What's the point?"** sounds so negative doesn't it? But it's how I felt and when you read it you can see its reasoning, the options and by the end it turns into something Positive for all to see. Not least "What else is there?" It relays hope.

**"The Ranting Post"** well this actually started as a blog. I wanted to get something off my chest. I started to write it down and then this Poem came out. And so its title describes exactly what it turned out to be. And the frustration of the "same old, same old" and although I have not got all the answers and have never said I do. I / we have had enough of politicians OF ALL PARTIES and their FAILURE in decades to make significant inroads to this damaging issue, to the victims, families and the society as a whole. Just look at the pathetic so called sentences some child abusers get. I have written to the PM and MP's. And a response I had even just about sentences just isn't the case. Telling me of the long sentences apparently judges can hand down. I'm sorry but for the rape and abuse of the most vulnerable in our society. There should be a minimum term. Untie their (Judges hands) or more to the point, stop using it as a reason or excuse for the status quo. At the end of the book I go into more detail about the PM letter found in this book. I as a victim, survivor or whatever you wish to know me as, ain't talking about stringing people up. I do not accept people abusing children and getting a couple of years. This is not good enough. And those in power WHO DO have the mandate to start a process of looking into, and changing sentences; have failed all of us, the Abused and the un-abused. I'm afraid it's that simple.

**"The Fantasist"** Well what's this one about then? Well the next extract was taken from a letter from a Community Mental Health Team to a GP (that I was under). It refers to some of the things that are insinuated against me that I didn't know about until I used the data protection act to get my Medical Records, from both a GP surgery and The Mental Health in 2008. It disgust's me. *"The concerns are related to the risk to myself and if John reaches a* *point where he is unable to differentiate between reality and fantasy."* The person who wrote this is a Psychiatric Nurse. So with these concerns, that unknown to me they had said at the time, they talked to me and helped me then? No. But the Slur continues. And that's what it is, especially when they never helped me and eventually turned me away. And discharged me from their care? Mmm. The list I speak of in the Poem refers to that long list of what Healthcare Professionals have said I have? and at the same time that I haven't? So as you can see its clear then? With all this going on, would you blame me for at least wanting to *Dream?* But this along with other Poems is a way to channel those emotions with creativity and being able to strike back WITHOUT being physical or verbally abusing to them, which only ever creates something they can use against you. Oh I know it's hard and I haven't always completely succeeded. And when I say channelling those emotions you do also have to remember many of these Poems where done a long time after the event. So I believe that just goes to show how important it still is years later to channel it out in the right way.

**"An Impression of Depression"** my main problem was never depression, at the beginning. But after not getting the right help it all just got compounded. Mixed with struggling with the Mental Health problems I did have. I soon became very low and depressed. I wrote this particular Poem because one morning I woke up and felt very low. I was experiencing some of those feelings you get, and I decided to jot down how I felt there and then. And so I wrote this Poem. But again it's not all negative (getting your feelings out never is, safely) but it takes you through the journey in this case literally within an hour. And by the end of it, it talks of coming out of the low back up to a sustainable high, and bearing up to face another day. Sometimes this can take longer. For some sadly they never quite make it and stay within this, in limbo which is very sad and deepens that lonely depressing feeling.

**"The Honesty of Love & the Ending of it"** nothing deep about this Poem and like in **"She Said / He Said"**, **"Up the Real Creek"** and **"The Two Sides to the Poet"** it's my attempt at a little light hearted humour. If I've failed I guess that's one laugh you can have on me. What led me to right it though, was I was watching something and I heard someone say "you're the best" (while they were in the act as it were) and I chuckled to myself thinking "Well they are hardly going to say you're the second best" so I wrote this. And I do want to purposefully try and write these sorts of Poems. I love those short amusing Poems. Not there yet myself, but trying.

133

**"To Who and Why"** I had just received a response from someone yet again I never wrote to, The Department for Children Schools and Families, on behalf of the Prime Minister. I sat there uploading the letter to my website. And I was typing my response to it. I found myself saying again and again "I'm writing to the Prime Minister" I even wrote that I felt a writing coming on and that if I did do something later I would call it "I am Writing to The Prime Minister" so the repetitiveness of this Poem is actually the point 10 Downing Street, mirroring the repetitiveness from you, of, same old same old.

**"Behind Closed Doors"** This is about the Secret Family Courts. Who behind closed doors take peoples children away. This is not my field but has, in 2008 & 2009 been brought to my attention by two campaigners. Firstly let me say. If people abuse their children then the state clearly has a duty to them, and does sometimes have to take them into care. There is No argument there from me. But what gets to me about this subject is, there have been sad cases where no one stepped in and a child died having been seen by Police, Social workers and more we have all seen these stories. You hear they sustained countless injuries, known to the services, yet no one acted. But then you can get the other extreme. Where some people have had their children taken away from them, yet they have NOT abused their children. Even worse, it's done behind closed doors. And if they make a mistake how can it be rectified? Who's hiding from what? You can protect people's identities without secret hearings. Secret Courts or Hearings are undemocratic. If this were connected with National Security then I'd reconsider. I want to know what's being done in my name, and who it's protecting.

**"Consumed Within"** some of the repetitive behaviour I have endured especially in the last two years, feeling like your climbing up the walls. As it says reading a Poem I just wrote for instance and finding I'm trapped reading it over and over most of or all day, stuck in a mentally painful loop.

**"Dead Poets"** snooty about Poetry? Then you won't like why I wrote this. As many people know there are too many in the Arts whether that be painting art forms or Poetry who really are doing significant damage to the arts. What gets me is. Some of them yes keep Dead Poets alive by re using and showing their works, nothing wrong with that. But at the same time creating a problem that others will have to solve in a hundred years or so. And that is there are *real Poets alive today*. And there are many who are just so snooty about

Poetry, that you can't even get a look in, in THEIR poetry world. One day in a hundred years or so someone will have to revive the Poets that are alive today, because their work wasn't appreciated when they were alive. We can and need to have both. I myself pay my own way. I don't get subsidized. And I have never asked for it. All I want is for these people and organisations to not stand IN OUR WAY and hinder us. That's all. I wrote to Arts Council England about this. Telling them I was fed up of going to sites displaying their logo that are not helping us. Why should those organisations get help from the Arts when they are censoring the Arts which is, as anyone knows, against Art itself. But don't worry the more I am pushed away, the more I have to say and the more I understand how important it is for it to be said.

**"The Rock"** I made a video of this Poem for my Bsafe1stalways YouTube account and website. It's been dedicated to NAPAC from me, with official kind consent. But I would also like to add to anyone who is breaking the Silence, Speaking out and Raising Awareness of the issues involved.

**"She Said / He Said"** This Poem came about because I was daydreaming about some woman I know. She is a real snooty person. But what gets me is there were times I could get on with her as good as I have with anyone. But then other times this other side came out and she was unpleasant, even belittling vulnerable people's problems, which is what led me to not be around her anymore. And as I sat there, knowing she didn't know anything about the child Abuse and the fact that I write. I imagined her reaction to knowing this. And I thought, I bet she'd find a way of being real snooty about it. And that's what this describes. And I like it because it's a fun Poem and I'd love to write more like this.

**"Within The Silence"** speaks again about the Silence. This is because I believe it's a good way of expressing myself, but also raising awareness of child abuse and the consequences in later life. The latter is personally what I'm interested in doing. I feel this is a very powerful Poem that touches the areas I just spoke of, but hopefully engages people into the issues involved.

**"The Other Side of Silence"** After writing the above Poem I really wanted to write something about the other side, hence the name. So this one is dedicated to all those who beat themselves up over what they should have done, even though they didn't know. And so couldn't have helped. Unlike the one above that just came to me, I did make a point of writing this one.

135

Wanting to Air the voice and silence of, not just the abused but in this case the many that haven't been abused. Who need to be heard just as much as us. I am a firm believer in trying to engage with each other, Child Abuse is a blot on us all. And it is painful for those decent people who wish like us to end it, and who share in our sorrow that it happens to anyone. I acknowledge this.

**"Blooming Vera"** I'm very proud of this Poem. This is my first Commissioned Work (Free) and the first Poem that was used on the radio, though more has now followed. It was mentioned to me that a radio show was being done on Dame Vera Lynn and they were interested in using a Poem about her. I knew, because like many I have always been moved by songs like "We'll Meet Again" and "There Will Always Be an England" for instance, that I could make a connection to her and her work. I jotted a couple of things down, watched some videos, and within forty eight hours. It started to come out. It was two a.m. I went to bed and at about two thirty a.m. I was writing what became "Blooming Vera" And when I read it to the station director (who loved it) he asked to put it on their website, which they did straight away. I was then also asked to do a recording of me reciting it for their show, to be aired Christmas day 2009. And so my Poetry was again being aired and as I said, I am very proud and pleased with it.

**"So Sad WAS I"** I rang The Samaritans about four times a few years ago. A wonderful experience as I hope this Poem expresses. Also important for me to add, the weird thing was I never rang them when I was at my worst, but having said that I was low when I did. It was beautiful hearing a voice of compassion and understanding when I was not getting it in my life. I again hope the Poem shows this. And at the back of the book you will see their number and web address (With NAPAC's and others). If you want to talk to someone, please do. And as a first port of call, it's not a bad start.

**"The Lost and Fallen"** lets learn something from those losses and the fallen. I have, others have and that's what this Poem is about. And I hope it celebrates their lives too. Doing what you can to make sure it's not all for nothing is something I know myself and know how precious it is. They are not lost because they are not forgotten, and never will be brushed aside by us. And most importantly, we won't let them be brushed aside by anyone. And those who head up the campaigns can show that. There will always be someone speaking for them, through us and us through someone else. TOGETHER, and in these circumstances sharing one voice.

**"If Not Now"** I live in the real world, but it's just so sad to see so many losing their lives. And it seems we hear that this one or that one is to prevent the next one. Yet we live in a world of it. What saddens me is how quick even a peaceful people can turn to war. You may well have victors, but who wages war and suffers NO LOSS?

**"Loves Not Lost On Me", "Love" and" Love Is..."** There's that four letter word again. Bunching these three together and showing its still there. "Love" and "Love Is" are expressing the many things and parts to love within me and others too. And I'm glad these Poems are also of my most recent and therefore at the end of this book. In dealing with all the issues you have read, if not been through yourself, it's still there. That tells us of its power and its meaning. It's so difficult I know. But that doesn't mean, at least once in a while I can't face it and acknowledge it's true, like now. **"Our Saviour"** talked of what hate and bitterness can do. My problems not so much hate anymore but it is bitterness. It's a demon I will have to overcome... with what? Love, has to be. It just has to be the answer, but love of what? Oh people, the hardest of them all for us. And you know as I write this not easily, but you who have been through all this, I bet you know the answer to my question. And it is for ME and YOU. Oh yeah... its love of us, love of ourselves. Maybe a long way away, but that's the one. And most of us would rather walk on broken glass or across hot Coles, than do that. But I tell you it's there. And when I'm not so well it's not something I want to acknowledge. But we deserve this Love. It's painful yes. I know the closest I came to not being here and the deepest pain I felt was when I believed I didn't deserve it. I was someone, and I tried to care about myself. And when people did more damage, it's why I stopped, or maybe you hide it to protect it. Either way it's there. Loves not lost on me, it's not lost on you because it's not lost. It's been hidden. I hope one day it won't just be **"Our Saviour"**... but yours too.

# PM (page 62) & Why Campaign?

As I mentioned in the introduction after many years of not getting the help I needed, I started to complain locally at first with those responsible and their superiors. Nothing changed. I then took it outside the local area with and to Independent organisations like the CAB, ICAS, The Healthcare Commission and many more. Nothing changed. I then took it to legal people; mostly sadly I couldn't even get a foot in the door, to coin a phrase. Not surprisingly... Nothing changed. I did all of this while my health deteriorated at times with four admissions into hospital and while being in some incredibly vulnerable situation's. But after doing all I could with the complaints procedures and using all the organisations purporting to be there for us. Nothing had changed and in the end and after over a decade I started to take it to among others Politician's.

Starting with the letter entitled PM found in this book I sent out in April 2008 to the Prime Minister Gordon Brown. I copied it to (and stating I wanted their opinion) to opposition MP's including David Cameron of The Conservatives, Nick Clegg of The Liberal Democrats, Alex Salmond of The SNP, Ieuan Win Jones of Plaid Cymru, Ian Paisley of The Democrat Unionist Party, Sylvia Harmon of The Ulster Unionist Party and Gerry Adams of Sinn Fein. I wrote this letter when Tony Blair was still Prime Minister but I was not able to complete and send it. But as it was still as relevant when Gordon Brown became Prime Minister I managed to get it together and send it. I purposefully chose these MP's to try and get a more representative opinion of The United Kingdom's Politician's. And I did. Most simply didn't even acknowledge it let alone reply.

My situation didn't change and in 2009 I continued to write to Politician's and The Prime Minister. Nothing has changed. I still wait for a response from The Prime Minister (as of January 2010). In 2009 I also started my website *www.bsafe1stalways.com* I continue to campaign and write to the government for a truly accountable system, and for change. If you would like to learn more please look up my website, to give you a quick glimpse of what I have been doing and trying to achieve in the long run. I hope you will see (added to the Poems and Prose in this book) what happens to some of us. In your name, as well as mine and sadly paid for, by a*ll* of us. But not just in financial terms... there *is* a human cost.

Together with others we are continuing to campaign, and will in the future. I hope you will support us even if it's just in thought. The lack of accountability for those who fail us within the system continually, is not just the reason why it continues, but sometimes a major factor in why it occurs at all. And that's why it is so important for those in power to force through changes. And as they are clearly not doing or achieving this, it is important that above all else that we expose this. If you feel strongly there are many ways you can join in, maybe you can write to your local MP or The Prime Minister. Just the once is enough to at least let them know how *you* feel. But if in spirit you are with us. Then thank you. John.

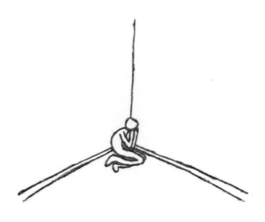

"The Child & the Full Room"

# "What was so special about 2009?"

It was a very important year for me because there were so many *Positive firsts* including:-

*Setting up my website* www.Bsafe1stalways.com about myself and Child Abuse issues, it has also branched out from there on YouTube, Twitter, Face book and MySpace. But my website is my main focus.

*First time my work was in Print* when one of my Pictures was used in a newsletter. One day the NAPAC newsletter came through my door. At that moment I was feeling a bit low. I opened the letter, and again but positively NAPAC brought tears to my eyes, yet more recognition. You know sometimes it's like. I have suffered; it's not dwelling on it, as so often it's not recognised. But this time it was.

*First time my work was in an Online Magazine* where more of my Pictures, A Poem and a well received review of my website was included. This was done by Survivor's Poetry a charity. Their magazine is free it's called "Poetry Express". I was quite taken back by the genuine thought that had gone into the review. It was more encouragement that I am on the right track, that's for sure.

*I Read five of my Poems to a live audience at a Rally in London* which was the first time. I have been longing to do this. I had such a drive to constructively speak out. And I did, along with others. I also made some good contacts and friends from others trying to make a difference to ourselves and each other.

*First use of My Poetry on the Radio* including:- *My First Commissioned work* was done, I did my *First Interview* & I Read three of My Poems which was *used on Air another first.* All these steps count. You may well be an exception and jump to the front. But the journey is what it's all about, I believe. Where do I start about this? I emailed different Radio Stations and a few presenters. I very quickly received two positive responses back.

An internet radio station contacted me first. They were interested if I had or could write something on either Dame Vera Lynn or Elvis Presley. This as I wrote before led me to write "Blooming Vera". But not mentioned yet is the fact the second person who contacted me was Tony Stringfellow who is an Author and Poet as well as being a radio presenter. I then did an interview with Tony on his "Page One" show, the format of the show being Poetry and literature. I have to say I had a great experience, not always the case when Abuse victims are interviewed (a view not lost on others too). Tony used the show to yes promote Poetry but also be respectful of the issues involved i.e. Child Abuse. There were no losers that day. I was interviewed in between reading three Poems. It lasted just over half an hour. Those interested can still hear this on my website, thanks again to Tony for consent to its use.

But you know strangest of all, these last two years I have struggled with my health. I've been very isolated. Yet this has all happened. I think this shows how much I do try, and how much I do want to better myself and my situation.

All I achieved in 2009 followed a first I achieved in 2008, which was the *first time I had any of my work published online.* So I've done well considering all what I have achieved I have done so in only just over a year. It was only then that I even tried to get anything published or out there for public viewing. Though I have to tell myself this sometimes when I doubt myself which is often. But luckily the facts help, when I look at it.

There's one last first in 2009 that's totally not related to Abuse or Poetry but worth a mention. *I did voluntary work* four days a week for eight months. This was with the British Red Cross. I would recommend this to any one with the time. And there are so many causes and not just charities you can get involved with and in. I met some genuine people including other volunteers, but members of the public too. It was definitely something I'd always wanted to do if I had the time. And clearly I did. And it was so worth it.

141

# FINAL WORDS

What of 2010 and onwards? Well I have already started with more of the same. On the 1st of January **"The Mover"** was played throughout New Years Day. It was a fun introduction to an Elvis Presley Marathon on *Radio Bracknell Forest* that I did. The interview I did on *Wolverhampton Community Radio* was also aired again within two weeks of the New Year. And more Radio is planned of which interest in showing more of my work was already shown in 2009.

The Poetry is still coming out after only three weeks of the year I've already written five new Poems:- **"The Humble Phoenix", "The Psychiatric Window", "Geezer Non Poet", "The Two Sides to the Poet" & "Cradle Me".** I want to, and have started to write more Poetry about other subject matter. I would like to write some more amusing Poems and to write of happier times. But with all that said and done, I must stay true to myself. And I think you will see in what I write, that's one thing I do do.

I already know that 2010 will bring another first, *Publishing this book.* And I am trying to make that one of many more firsts like before. I'm still trying to have my Poetry published in a mainstream paper formatted Poetry Magazine, after submitting to four without success in 2009.

I'm continuing to build on what I have achieved in the last two years, to re-enforce it and back it all up. I will do more Poetry reading and I have plans to do an open mike night and more at other venues when I can (check on my website to find out more). I am discussing with others of how we can promote ourselves and each other. Because many of us still believe we are not being heard, and changes are needed. So I haven't finished Campaigning for True Accountability within the system, and airing their and our silence. So the Prime Minister and others will be hearing from me again soon.

And finally and as always, I'm trying to leave something of worth behind, for the day I stop. And in so doing fulfil my main goal. To make sure, no matter what has happened to me, *that it's not all for nothing.* That really would be something. And remember...

*Money comes and goes. What you feel, you will take with you.*

THE END?

OH NO IT'S JUST THE BEGINNING

LET'S NOT END IT IN DEATH
LET'S BEGIN IT WITH LIFE
SO THAT WHEN DEATH DOES COME
WE CAN SAY, WE DID LIVE

www.Bsafe1stalways.com

# Some useful contacts and information:-

Disclaimer. I cannot vouch for all material on these sites, but I have had positive experiences from them myself. As always with these issues please take care of yourself and be aware of the content triggering you, or the disturbing information you may come across. *B Safe 1st always.*

**The Samaritans.** If you are in crisis, or need urgent help or advice, please contact The Samaritans on 08457 909 090 or you can go to http://www.samaritans.org/

**The National Association for People Abused in Childhood.** You can call their Free phone support line on 0800 085 3330 or you can go to http://www.napac.org.uk/

**Survivor's Poetry.** Is a charity encouraging the Poetry of Survivors of Abuse and Mental Distress, they have an online magazine which is downloadable for FREE and there is a forum on the site too. http://www.survivorspoetry.com

**British Red Cross.** I did voluntary work for them, but yes there are plenty of other organisations that you could be involved with. http://www.redcross.org.uk/index.asp?id=39992

**B Safe 1st Always.** This is my website which is trying to Raise Awareness of Child Abuse and the Consequences in Later Life. http://www.bsafe1stalways.com I also have a presence elsewhere. But if you go to the Links / Books Page on my website you can see other useful websites and books by Survivors of Childhood Abuse.

**The Data Protection Act.** I found this page was useful to help get started on gaining information held about me. http://en.wikipedia.org/wiki/Data_Protection_Act_1998

**Just enjoy Poetry?** Then try out Tony Stringfellow's "Page One" Show on WCR FM. To find out more follow this Link http://wcrt.entadsl.com/cmsms/index.php?page=tony-stringfellow or you can find Tony on MySpace.

**Don't forget your local Library.** O.K. I know there's the internet, but please don't forget it's a tried and tested resource.

I've just put a couple of useful numbers for a start. I'm sure if you contacted some of the above they could refer you on to someone if they couldn't help.

## Acknowledgements: -

On page 22 there's a reference to:- "Judge Not" – Robert Marley 1962 – Island records. The song can be found on the Bob Marley 'Songs of Freedom' 4 CD set. There is also a quote from the Star Trek movie 'First Contact' Paramount Pictures.

*All internal and Cover Art and Designs by John Harrison Copyright 2010*

144

# Thank You

My acknowledgement

of you